The Te

THE
TENTH JUSTICE

THE SOLICITOR GENERAL
AND THE RULE OF LAW

BY

LINCOLN CAPLAN

VINTAGE BOOKS

A DIVISION OF RANDOM HOUSE   NEW YORK

First Vintage Books Edition, December 1988

Grateful acknowledgment is made to the following for
permission to reprint previously published material: *Thomas
Barr:* Excerpts from "Statement by the Lawyers' Committee for
Civil Rights Under Law," June 4, 1985, by Thomas Barr et al.
Reprinted by permission of Thomas Barr. *Archibald Cox:*
Excerpts from the lecture "Storm Over the Supreme Court,"
given at Hunter College in 1985. Reprinted by permission.
Harvard Law School Library: Excerpt from a Memorandum
dated March 8, 1933, by Felix Frankfurter, from the Felix
Frankfurter Papers, Harvard Law School Library. Reprinted by
permission.

Portions of this book originally appeared in *The New Yorker,* the
Washington Post, and the *Baltimore Sun.*

Library of Congress Cataloging-in-Publication Data
Caplan, Lincoln.
The tenth justice.
Bibliography: p.
Includes index.
1. United States.   Solicitor General.
2. Government attorneys—United States.   3. Rule of
law—United States.   I. Title.
KF8793.C36 1988   347.73'16   88-40048
ISBN 0-394-75955-9   347.30716

Manufactured in the United States of America

10 9 8 7 6 5 4 3 2 1

For Susan

For Susan

Contents

Solicitors General
of the United States

Name	Term	President
Benjamin H. Bristow	October 1870–November 1872	Grant
Samuel F. Phillips	November 1872–May 1885	Grant
John Goode	May 1885–August 1886	Cleveland
George A. Jenks	July 1886–May 1889	Cleveland
Orlow W. Chapman	May 1889–January 1890	Harrison
William Howard Taft	February 1890–March 1892	Harrison
Charles H. Aldrich	March 1892–May 1893	Harrison
Lawrence Maxwell, Jr.	April 1893–January 1895	Cleveland
Holmes Conrad	February 1895–July 1897	Cleveland
John K. Richards	July 1897–March 1903	McKinley
Henry M. Hoyt	February 1903–March 1909	Roosevelt
Lloyd Wheaton Bowers	April 1909–September 1910	Taft
Frederick W. Lehmann	December 1910–July 1912	Taft
William Marshall Bullitt	July 1912–March 1913	Taft
John William Davis	August 1913–November 1918	Wilson
Alexander C. King	November 1918–May 1920	Wilson
William L. Frierson	June 1920–June 1921	Wilson
James M. Beck	June 1921–June 1925	Harding
William D. Mitchell	June 1925–March 1929	Coolidge
Charles Evans Hughes, Jr.	May 1929–April 1930	Hoover
Thomas D. Thacher	March 1930–May 1933	Hoover
James Crawford Biggs	May 1933–March 1935	Roosevelt
Stanley Reed	March 1935–January 1938	Roosevelt
Robert H. Jackson	March 1938–January 1940	Roosevelt
Francis Biddle	January 1940–September 1941	Roosevelt
Charles Fahy	November 1941–September 1945	Roosevelt
J. Howard McGrath	October 1945–October 1946	Truman

Name	Term	President
Philip B. Perlman	July 1947–August 1952	Truman
Walter J. Cummings, Jr.	December 1952–March 1953	Truman
Simon E. Sobeloff	February 1954–July 1956	Eisenhower
J. Lee Rankin	August 1956–January 1961	Eisenhower
Archibald Cox	January 1961–July 1965	Kennedy
Thurgood Marshall	August 1965–August 1967	Johnson
Erwin N. Griswold	October 1967–June 1973	Johnson
Robert H. Bork	June 1973–January 1977	Nixon
Wade H. McCree	March 1977–August 1981	Carter
Rex Lee	August 1981–June 1985	Reagan
Charles Fried	October 1985–	Reagan

Author's Note

This paperback edition contains a new Foreword, some additional comments in A Note on Sources, and other minor changes to the original text. Otherwise, the edition presents the book as it first appeared in hardcover. I researched and wrote the book during most of 1985, 1986, and part of 1987. It reflects my findings and points of view during that period.

—Lincoln Caplan
August 1988

Foreword
to the Vintage Edition

DURING 1987, THE rule of law was of paramount concern in the United States. The celebration of the Constitution's bicentennial was energetic and widespread, and it was deepened by the unexpected and, for many Americans, riveting events of the Congressional hearings about the Iran-Contra affair and on Robert Bork's nomination to the Supreme Court. The outcomes of those hearings—the conclusion by the majority of the members of the Iran-Contra committees that the Reagan Administration had displayed "disdain for the law" in the affair, and the Senate's rejection of the Bork nomination by a vote of fifty-eight to forty-two, the largest margin in American history—prompted many contradictory reactions. But whatever one's views of these outcomes, it seems safe to observe that the intensity of these responses underscored how much the law matters in this country.

Of the year's developments in the law, it is difficult to pick which was the most notable. The Iran-Contra affair is a prime candidate, because of the corruption of the processes of government that it revealed and the renewed pledge to honor democratic principles that it prompted. Corruption can take many forms, whether the old-fashioned kind involving misuse of influence and office, abuse of the processes by which laws are made, enforced, and interpreted, or gross distortion of ideas at the heart of constitutional law. Under this broad definition, the Iran-Contra affair can be grouped with the Wedtech affair. These cases, together with the extraordinary number of Reagan officials involved in scandal of all kinds, begin to suggest our contemporary experience of lawlessness and its social costs. Seen in this light, I believe, the

Iran-Contra affair ranks with Watergate in the gravity of its challenge to the American system of government.

But in some ways, the debate over the Bork nomination and the public clamor about it were even more important. That controversy can be analyzed from many vantage points, but one seems especially significant now, some months after the defeat of the nomination. For the first time, the Bork controversy revealed to citizens outside the legal world a breakdown in legal consensus—a breakdown that had become familiar to legal scholars in recent years. This public revelation goes to the heart of the meaning of the rule of law in our democracy, and to issues at the core of this book.

THE RULE OF LAW has had three key dimensions since the start of the Republic. To begin with, there is the structure of the government as established by the Constitution. Its three branches were designed to check and balance each other, for the Framers of the Constitution recognized that unbridled power in any one branch would jeopardize the government's overall equilibrium. As the third and "least dangerous" branch, in Alexander Hamilton's phrase, the Supreme Court came to be judged especially responsible for shaping the law, as the final arbiter in legal disputes between the branches and between the citizens and the government.

Then, there are the substantive contents of the Constitution. Besides establishing the structure of the government, that document provides the ultimate authority for resolving legal differences. The traditional view about the contents of the Constitution—that its meaning is neither fixed nor self-explanatory—was explained in 1949 by Edward Levi (who became Attorney General in the Ford Administration) in a legal classic called *An Introduction to Legal Reasoning*. "The Constitution in its general provisions embodies the conflicting ideals of the community," Levi wrote. "Who is to say what these ideals mean in any definite way?" Not the Framers, because words they chose were often "ambiguous." Not any one Supreme Court, because "an appeal can always be made back to the Constitution." Levi concluded that the Constitution's "words change to receive the content which the community gives them."

This change in "words" has occurred through legal reasoning—through the Supreme Court's interpretation of the text, structure, and history of the Constitution, and of prior Court rulings, and of the experience of the nation. Because the meaning of the Constitution is neither fixed nor self-explanatory, it has been vital that legal reasoning be marked by its own integrity. Without the law's internal accountability, the whole system of government would have collapsed long ago.

Legal reasoning is the black box of the law. As scholars often note, it is sometimes possible to have two able judges apply the same law to the same set of facts and reach opposite conclusions about the proper outcome in the case at hand. But, to Levi, each field of the law, including constitutional law, is made up of different rules of reasoning that give it some coherence and enable it to contribute to the law's general purpose of lending predictability and stability to society. It is no exaggeration to say that consistent legal reasoning has been essential to American governance. Whether one is liberal or conservative, being true to a vision of a lawful society has required that lawyers express their commitment through careful legal reasoning. Legal reasoning has supplied the third essential ingredient to the rule of law.

THESE ELEMENTS of the rule of law have always been subject to evolution in this country. Two hundred years ago, the Constitution was seen as a document with contradictory effects: it established the government of the United States, but severely constrained the government's actions. If the government sought to do something that would impinge on the lives of citizens, it had to justify its action by citing the constitutional passage that gave it the authority to do so. In the past generation, when we have long since taken for granted the Constitution's energizing force, the government has confirmed one of James Madison's deep fears. The power of Congress and of the President have spread enormously, and in a profound shift in the burden of responsibility, those powers have usually been checked only when a citizen convinces a court that one of the political branches has violated a constitutional right.

The Supreme Court is charged with the duty of protecting

citizens from unlawful coercion by the government—and especially of protecting unpopular minorities from the tyranny of the majority—by applying the guarantees in the Bill of Rights. As the political branches expanded their authority, the Court could be expected to be asked to resolve an increasing number of cases dealing with civil rights and liberties, and it was. When the political branches failed to solve major social problems affecting civil rights—racial discrimination is the most prominent example—it also followed that the Court would be asked to tackle them, and it did.

To address these problems, the Court relied on what Justice Lewis Powell in 1987 called "an evolving concept" of the Constitution. In the heyday of this activism, as I describe in more detail in this book, conservatives like Felix Frankfurter cautioned the Court about expanding its authority too far, and tried to restrain the Court by promoting conservative practices of legal reasoning. But Frankfurter and other conservatives joined their liberal colleagues in believing that the Constitution was a living charter relevant to these social problems, and that its meaning had to grow as the country faced and tried to solve its contemporary social dilemmas.

Contrary to what some contemporary legal conservatives contend, the techniques of reasoning that traditional conservatives favored did not compel blind obedience to liberal judicial precedents. Traditional legal reasoning was often used to challenge liberal precedents, and in recent years has been relied on by the Burger Court to moderate some Warren Court decisions. (A good example of this is the series of subsequent rulings that limit the effect of the 1966 Miranda decision, guaranteeing certain rights to criminal suspects.) But these techniques of legal reasoning have reflected the judgment that once a basic question in the law has been resolved and has become part of the legal fabric, and is supported by a national consensus, it should be widely honored. (In the case of Miranda, the Court's ruling was originally criticized by the police; by and large, it is now welcomed.)

THE VIEWS about constitutional law that Robert Bork presented to the Senate were at odds with long-dominant assumptions about each of these key ingredients of the rule of law. As a critic of the "Imperial Judiciary," he had contended that the Supreme Court must always defer to the will of the majority, as that will is expressed in Presidential decisions, Congressional statutes, and state law, except where the Constitution clearly states differently, or else it robs the majority of the most basic liberty in a democracy—the liberty to enact the will of the majority. As a believer in "original intent," Bork had argued that, when justices look outside the text and structure of the Constitution to find the meaning of that document, their judgments are constrained by nothing but personal values—constrained, in his view, by nothing at all.

As to legal reasoning, while Bork told the Senate that a "judge must give great respect for precedent," he made clear that his expressions of this respect were likely to be quite limited if he became a justice. He might not have aggressively overturned precedent, but he was unlikely to extend the reasoning and reach of prior decisions as traditional conservatives had done. His grounds for this reluctance were identical with the arguments often stated by the Reagan Administration in its attacks on the "liberal" judiciary: if the Court were strictly bound by established law, it would end up only strengthening decisions of the past generation that Ronald Reagan and Robert Bork considered wrong.

If the Constitution's provisions were as clear-cut as some of the language used by Bork to state his views, it would be hard to understand the gap between his model of constitutional government and the one that has prevailed for the last thirty years. During his testimony before the Senate Judiciary Committee, however, Bork indicated the extent to which his view of "original intent" was not so much a formula for interpreting the Constitution as it was a theory about the balance of power in American government.

In response to questioning by Senator Arlen Specter, a Republican from Pennsylvania, Bork acknowledged that the Constitution's key provisions and amendments, like the Fourteenth Amendment's guarantees of equal protection and due process, are rarely plain about their meaning. In effect, Bork admitted that all jurists, conservative or liberal, must look beyond the Constitution's words to help determine the document's meaning.

Given this acknowledgment, it is not surprising that a liberal like Justice William Brennan used language similar to Bork's in describing how the Supreme Court should draw meaning from the Constitution. "We never consciously put something there that shouldn't be there," Brennan told an interviewer in 1987. "We find it in the Constitution or within the basic purpose of a given clause."

The difference between a Brennan and a Bork is marked by how they would use the various tools and techniques of reasoning about the Constitution. For Brennan, especially where the intent of the Framers about a provision is ambiguous, the acceptable and useful guides for interpreting it must include the provision's purpose, the Court's prior decisions, and the experience of the nation.

For Bork, this evolutionary approach to the law—what Felix Frankfurter called the need to put meaning *into* the Constitution—has led American law to a dangerous impasse—"a tipping point for democracy," Bork has called it. He sought to save the American government from what he described as the "tyranny of the minority," and return the government to the balance that he contended the Framers designed. To this end, he advocated cutting back the role of the Supreme Court and the lower federal courts.

Between 1982 and 1987, Bork tried to do just this in some of his opinions as an appeals-court judge. He challenged basic doctrines (about the separation of powers, for example) and more technical-sounding ones (about access of individuals to the courts). With another colleague in the majority for whom he wrote the opinion, he put aside forty years of sustained precedent that led to an outcome he didn't like (in a case about rate-setting by utilities). He chose to reach far beyond the issue before him as a judge, "to conduct a general spring-cleaning of constitutional law," according to the disapproving judges who otherwise concurred with his decision about the narrow question before them (whether the Navy could exclude homosexuals from its ranks). For seventy-five years, the debate about the constitutional right of privacy focused on the scope of that right. Bork set himself apart as a jurist by questioning the right's very existence. In his academic theorizing and his actions as a judge, Bork, in effect, called for a major redefinition of the rule of law.

THE BORK HEARINGS may have exaggerated the differences of opinion in current constitutional thinking. Congressional hearings have their limits, and heated ones often underscore discord rather than harmony. The Bork hearings were treated by some as a referendum on the Reagan Administration's extreme arguments on the need to redress the balance of power in government. In speeches by Attorney General Edwin Meese, the Administration gave short shrift to the authority of Congress, expanded the power of the President by fiat, and challenged the accepted premise that it is the province and duty of the Supreme Court to interpret statutes and the Constitution, and say what the law is. Robert Bork's writing about constitutional law is plentiful and, as even Bork supporters observed, filled with invective. His writings seemed to make it hard for participants to follow the judge's own advice that they should "lower their voices" in discussion of the law.

Despite the disagreements expressed at the hearings, there were participants, including members of the Senate Judiciary Committee, who concluded that the outcome of the Bork hearings was a form of consensus; they saw the "country" as having expressed general agreement about the importance and good sense of the civil-rights laws passed by Congress in the 1960s, and of some civil-rights decisions made by the Supreme Court during the Warren Court era and after. As a distinguished witness later put it, "The constitutional center held."

In that view, the nomination had been defeated because Robert Bork had opposed the one-person, one-vote standard that brought democratic reform to elections, especially in the South. He had opposed the Court's decision striking down poll taxes and its grounds for finding that women must be given equal protection under the law. He had opposed the Court's broad protection of free speech and offered a far more restrictive standard. He had opposed the Supreme Court decision allowing public institutions to use affirmative-action remedies to redress the effects of racial discrimination.

Attorney General Meese later asserted that only "anti-intellectualism" could account for the Senate Judiciary Committee's rejection of these views. Senators on the committee and in the full house of Congress who opposed the Bork nomination reached a different conclusion. Above all, many regarded the vote as a judgment about ideas, and considered it an affirmation of moral and social consensus.

THIS AFFIRMATION of consensus was significant, because it was in part about a dimension of the rule of law that Robert Bork had vigorously challenged—the role of the Supreme Court in American governance. Yet the consensus was also limited in an extremely important way. When particular Court decisions were at issue in the Bork hearings, what were agreed upon were results in social policy rather than constitutional reasoning, outcomes rather than the legal logic by which the Justices interpreted the Constitution to arrive at them.

Until the hearings, Edward Levi's description of how constitutional law is made might have been said to define the mainstream of American thinking. The Bork hearings were so divisive on so many substantive issues of constitutional law that they left the wide impression that a mainstream no longer existed—that it had broken into many different currents. Bork's supporters (including Edward Levi) claimed the opposite, and declared Bork's views to be in the mainstream of legal thinking. But, at a minimum, the wide range of opinions about the issues raised at the Bork hearings indicated that the reach of the premises underlying mainstream ideas, summed up almost two generations before by Levi, was increasingly limited, as was the group of adherents to those ideas; that other streams had broken off to the left and right; and that Bork was plainly to the right rather than in the center.

At the hearings, questions about the meaning of liberty in the Constitution were superseded by questions about whether that concept includes a general right to privacy, and panels of academic experts squared off about each of these disputes. By the time the hearings ended, it seemed that there was far more disagreement than agreement among the nation's legal scholars about how to read and apply the Constitution. Every time a question was raised about some key provision of the document, it seemed answerable only in stark, contradictory terms.

THE POLARIZATION over proper legal reasoning and the meaning of the rule of law at its most abstract, yet fundamental, level reflected the polarization that Robert Bork's ideas had helped to create about the role of the Supreme Court. To key members of the Reagan Administration, this split was desirable, for it offered the American people a choice between boldly differentiated formulations of the role of law in our democratic society.

The Administration favored what it considered a required cutback in the role of the Court and a narrow reading of the Constitution. In the Administration's view, the only alternative approach was found in the prevailing commitment to an "imperial" Court, whose activities had expanded so far beyond what was contemplated in the Constitution that some of its landmark decisions were, in Robert Bork's terms, "lawless" and "pernicious."

To others—liberals, moderates, and some traditional conservatives—what the Administration judged anathema was merely the current state of the Court and its jurisprudence, in the normal, if sometimes combative, evolution of the constitutional order. What the Administration described as an approach mandated by "original intent" was in reality the expression of a divisive ideology.

Inadvertently, the Reagan team provided evidence that the latter view was correct. Early in 1988, the *Washington Post* reported, the Attorney General's office distributed a memorandum to senior officials at the Justice Department urging them to maintain the practice of provocation during the Administration's last months, to "polarize the debate" on prominent legal issues. "We must not seek 'consensus,' we must confront," the memorandum stated. To the Reagan team, polarization was a means and an end, not merely a negative side effect.

This was one reason Robert Bork appealed so strongly to the President's followers as a candidate for the Court, and why, after his defeat, he had their support when he resigned from his appellate-court seat. No longer restrained by judicial protocol, he could speak out against his critics, and proselytize for the vision of the Court and the Constitution that he and the Reagan Administration shared.

As the Bork hearings showed, the polarization that the Reagan Administration sought in the American legal community required the participation of the legal left as well as the right. The hearings provided consuming drama, in part because few who took part remained innocent of partisanship. Lawyers and scholars on both ends of the spectrum used accusatory, misleading language, sometimes treating the law as a forum for clever debate and controversy—an "intellectual feast," as Bork called it—instead of as a tool for solving problems in human affairs. The resolution of the surface drama of confirmation should not obscure that behind the bitter debate over the Bork nomination lay a crisis in the law.

D URING THE S UPREME C OURT'S 1985 Term, on which the second half of this book concentrates, the Solicitor General's office filed numerous briefs for the Reagan Administration that reflected this crisis. As Justices representing the legal left, center, and right seemed to go out of their way to observe in Court opinions, some of the SG's briefs misstated legislative history, judicial decisions, and other basic components of the law, in an effort to advance the President's social agenda.

Put differently, the Reagan Administration sometimes turned standard tools of legal reasoning into political devices rather than firm expressions of commitment to the rule of law. It spurned the idea that, for liberals and conservatives, taking issue with Supreme Court doctrine in order to be true to a vision of the law requires the use of consistent means, through the careful practice of legal reasoning.

This elementary misuse of the law was lost in the developing crisis that climaxed in 1987 with the Bork hearings, where the central question was not how to read the law as embodied in statutes or judicial decisions but how to interpret the Constitution. Because the briefs in which it put aside standard practices of legal reasoning sometimes dealt with cases where the Constitution was at stake, the Administration's misuse of the law was regarded by even some critics as what the Reagan team claimed—aggressive but appropriate participation in the legal debate about the meaning of the Constitution.

But if they were simply aggressive statements, the Administration's briefs were still harmful, for reasons that the Bork hearings eventually helped explain. The American system of government is distinguished by a need for the consent of the governed. The law is the compact between the people and their representatives, and the Congress, the Executive Branch, and the Supreme Court must forge legal consensus in this country. If they fail to achieve this, they stir confusion and frustration, and encourage disrespect— even contempt—for the law at the deepest level.

In the Reagan era, some of the President's devoted allies in Congress, some of his key representatives in the Executive Branch, and his prized nominee to the Supreme Court were so committed to what they considered the purity of their radical ideas—and some of the country's most influential legal thinkers were so adamant about the correctness of their conflicting views—that they eviscerated this consensus. They turned the law into a wedge and, in the case of the Administration in particular, willfully drove Americans apart.

Washington, D.C.
March 1988

The Tenth Justice

I

The Tenth Justice

THE UNITED STATES takes pride in its commitment to the rule of law, and during this century the individual who has best represented this dedication may be a little-known figure called the Solicitor General. The nation's constitutional government is distinguished by its need for the consent of the governed, and the law is the compact between the people and their representatives. Of all the nation's public officials, including the Attorney General and the Justices of the Supreme Court, the Solicitor General is the only one required by statute to be "learned in the law."[1] Although he serves in the Department of Justice, and his title, like the Attorney General's, is displayed in large bronze letters on the facade of the Department's building, he also has permanent chambers in the Supreme Court. The fact that he keeps offices at these two distinct institutions underscores his special role. The Solicitor General's principal task is to represent the Executive Branch of the government in the Supreme Court, and when he takes the lectern before the Justices, his status is clear. With his assistants and other lawyers for the government, the Solicitor General is among the last attorneys to carry on the custom of arguing at the Court in formal garb of striped pants, dark vest, and tails. The Justices expect the substance of his remarks to be distinguished as well. They count on him to look beyond the government's narrow interests. They rely on him to help guide them to the right result in the case at hand, and to pay close attention to the case's impact on the law.[2]

Because of what Justice Lewis Powell has described as the Solicitor's "dual responsibility"[3] to both the Judicial and the Executive Branch, he is sometimes called the Tenth Justice.[4] Although he operates in a sphere of government that is invisible to almost all citizens, his influence is undeniable. Some parts of it are not hard to measure. During the 1983 Term of the Supreme Court, of the 3,878 petitions for writs of certiorari (the form in which most parties ask the Court to review a case) submitted by lawyers across the country, the Justices granted only 3 percent. Of petitions from the Solicitor General, they approved 79 percent, or almost four out of five. Whenever the government supported a petition as amicus curiae, or friend of the Court, in a case where it was not directly involved, the chances that the Court would approve the petition rose from 2 percent to 78 percent—up thirty-nine times. The Solicitor General, unlike the ordinary legal counsel, appeared to have almost a standing invitation to come to the Court, and was able to bring along most advocates he sponsored. Once he arrived before the Court, he was even more effective. Of the 262 cases the Justices considered that Term, the government took part in 150. The Solicitor General (or SG, as he is called) won 83 percent of his cases outright and partial victories in another 2 percent, for an exceptional overall success rate of 85 percent. [5]

While the SG's performance has only rarely reached this level, [6] it has been remarkably better than the record of nongovernmental attorneys in almost every year since the SG became the government's chief lawyer and began to do what most people assume falls naturally to the Attorney General. Until 1853, the Attorney General's was a part-time job. He had a smaller salary than the other members of the President's Cabinet, and was expected to supplement his income through the cases that he attracted in private practice because of his office. The government's modest amount of legal business was then managed by lawyers who did not work for the Attorney General, and its court appearances in civil suits were dealt with by a Solicitor in the Department of the Treasury. [7]

In the mid-nineteenth century, as the country grew, the volume of official legal work expanded and became more than the government could handle. Private attorneys then took on the public's cases. But their judgments about the law were sometimes at odds with the government's, and their fees were high. As dissatisfaction with this arrangement spread, a congressional panel known as the Joint Committee on Retrenchment recommended that a Ministry of Justice be established to save money and consolidate the government's legal work under one master. The legislators also realized that the Attorney General was increasingly preoccupied with management and politics, and had little time for the intricacies of courtroom law.

In 1870, when Congress created the Justice Department, it drew on the model of Treasury's Solicitor and directed that "there shall be . . . an officer learned in the law, to assist the Attorney-General in the performance of his duties, to be called the solicitor-general. . . ."[8] Congressman Thomas Jenckes, a Republican from Rhode Island who sponsored the bill establishing the office, explained: "We propose to have a man of sufficient learning, ability, and experience that he can be sent to New Orleans or to New York, or into any court wherever the government has any interest in litigation, and there present the case of the United States as it should be presented."[9] Though early SGs tried occasional cases before juries (the first Solicitor was Benjamin Bristow, who had made his reputation prosecuting the Ku Klux Klan),[10] the people in the office have for many years concentrated on the government's appeals, especially to the Supreme Court.

In 1986, the Justice Department had 5,107 attorneys.[11] The SG's office had only twenty-three, the size of a small law firm. The Solicitor's team has always been relatively tiny, but within the Executive Branch the SG has played a powerful and almost judicial role consistent with his standing as the Tenth Justice. For every petition the SG sends to the Supreme Court, he rejects five from federal agencies with grievances they want the Justices to settle.[12] Often he spurns an agency's request because he thinks it is wrong about the law. (A Solicitor General once wrote, "Government lawyers, like those in general practice, may experience that marvelous adjustment of perspective which often comes to the most ardent advocate when he loses—that is, the realization that he really should have lost.")[13] Even if he thinks the agency is right, the SG is not easily persuaded to allow an appeal. As the then Associate Justice William Rehnquist noted with approval in a 1984 opinion, "The Solicitor General considers a variety of factors, such as the limited resources of the government and the crowded dockets of the courts, before authorizing an appeal." [14] If the facts of a case that the government has lost are so unusual as to give it little weight as a precedent, or if there is general agreement among the dozen regional U.S. Courts of Appeals about the law under scrutiny, the SG will usually accept the defeat.

Lawyers on the Solicitor's team prefer to talk about the cases they present to the Supreme Court, but they spend half their time sifting through proposed appeals from trial-court rulings against the government. [15] In a speech at the University of Oklahoma, one Solicitor General bragged, "If the district court in Oklahoma City makes a decision which the United States Attorney doesn't like, he may well tell the press, 'I am going to appeal.' When I see those statements in the press, I say to myself, 'Yes, he is going to appeal if I say he can.' But sometimes I don't." [16] The SG and his staff have a reputation for stinginess, and the trait matters because they are in effect a court of last resort. By screening cases that they believe are not ready for hearing by the Courts of Appeals or the Supreme Court, the Solicitor General and his aides help assure that judges rule on those the SG does consider ripe for appeal.

The SG's influence at the Supreme Court is even more striking than his authority within the Executive Branch. He does not sit beside the Justices on the bench, but he stands in place of them when he decides which cases should be taken to the Court. For all its dominance, the Supreme Court is a relatively passive institution: the Justices must wait for litigants to raise issues before they can address them. And they rely on the Solicitor General more than anyone else to help choose and present the most pressing matters for review. Not long before he died, in 1985, retired Justice Potter Stewart said that he and his colleagues regarded the SG as a "traffic cop," acting to control the flow of cases to the Court. [17]

It was William Howard Taft, a former SG himself, who, as Chief Justice, made the Solicitor so essential to the Justices on this count. Taft believed that citizens were entitled to one appeal, not two—the appeal they could take from a trial in federal court to a Circuit Court should end the government's duty to provide a safeguard against an unfair ruling in the lower court. [18] In 1925, he helped guide through Congress a law known as the Judges' Bill, which ended the Justices' duty to take almost every case appealed to them, and increased their discretion to select the cases they wanted to hear and let others rest as lower courts had decided. Once empowered to pick most of its cases, the Court relied on the SG to guide the choice.

The influence of the Solicitor at the Court goes beyond helping the Justices set their docket. The Justices also turn to the SG for help on legal problems that appear especially vexing, and two or three dozen times a year they invite him and his office to submit briefs in cases where the government is not a party.[19] In these cases especially, the Justices regard him as a counselor to the Court.[20] But in every case in which he participates, the Justices expect him to take a long view. The Solicitor General advises the Court about the meaning of federal statutes as well as about the Constitution, so his judgments regularly affect the work of the Legislature as much as the Executive and the Judiciary. Lawyers who have worked in the SG's office like to say that the Solicitor General avoids a conflict between his duty to the Executive Branch, on the one hand, and his respect for the Congress or his deference to the Judiciary, on the other, through a higher loyalty to the law.[21]

For many generations before the Reagan era, in both Democratic and Republican administrations, the Solicitor General more often than not met the standards of a model public servant— discreet, able, trustworthy. Most took him for granted. During the first six years of the present Administration, however, the role of the Solicitor General was transformed. The transformation went considerably beyond the normal, unexceptional differences in policy and approach that can naturally be expected to occur from one SG to the next. Instead, far-reaching changes were pushed through by Presidential Counsellor–turned–Attorney General Edwin Meese and Assistant Attorney General William Bradford Reynolds, two of the Administration's most powerful and controversial officials; the changes were resisted by Rex Lee, the Administration's first SG, who returned to private practice and to the teaching of law at Brigham Young University; they were carried out by Lee's successor, Charles Fried; and they were at the center of many of the deep, near-seismic reforms that the Reagan Administration tried to bring about in American law.

II

Lore

IN A CORRIDOR on the fifth floor of the Justice Department, where the lawyers in the SG's office work, photographs of thirty-six of the thirty-eight men who have served as Solicitor General hang in a kind of gallery. Aside from one in color and a sepia-toned print whose border seems tinged with gold, the photos are black-and-white. Like the reputation of the archetypical SG, the subjects of the pictures appear direct, upright, and somehow eccentric. Almost half wear mustaches. None is a woman, and two—Supreme Court Justice Thurgood Marshall and former appeals court judge Wade McCree—are black. Their average tenure has been three years.

Except for a few articles in law reviews, occasional mentions in books about other legal topics, and speeches by Solicitors reprinted in bar journals, little has been written about the SG. The history of the Solicitor General is passed on among the small circle of lawyers who know about it—usually by moving down the line of men pictured in the gallery and telling stories of what they and their teams contributed to the office. The stories are then retold to a new SG or lawyer in the office so he will know the tradition he's expected to uphold.[1]

By most accounts, John W. Davis, who was SG from 1913 through 1918, was one of the truly distinguished Solicitors. He was then appointed Ambassador to Great Britain (in 1918), and ran for President (in 1924), but while he was SG he made the job more prestigious than the Attorney General's.[2] As soon as Davis began his first argument before the Supreme Court as Solicitor General, Chief Justice Edward White sighed in relief: the government's brief was in good hands. As SG, Davis often took long walks with the Chief Justice, who used the chance to remind Davis about the Court's reliance on him. White generally did not say much about himself, but one day he stopped, planted his feet, and said, "You know, Mr. Davis, I'm not an educated man. Everything I get I've got to get through my ears. If you say that something happened in 1898, and the next time you say it happened in 1888, why Sir, it's just as if you'd stuck a knife in me!"[3]

Thomas Thacher, SG from 1930 through 1933, perfected a technique that became an insider's signal of the Solicitor's views. Thacher had given up one judgeship to take the job, and subsequently filled another judgeship, and, perhaps because of his judicial temperament, he was reluctant to sign briefs whose legal validity he doubted; but he was also unwilling, on the other hand, to withhold from the Supreme Court arguments he could not fully discredit. In close cases, he decided, he would sign the government's brief, but tag on a disclaimer that became known among the SG's lawyers as "tying a tin can." "The foregoing is presented as the position of the Internal Revenue Service," the brief would clatter, letting the Justices know it was not the Solicitor General's view. Since the Court rarely subscribes to the arguments of a brief from any part of the government without the SG's sponsorship, the judgment that Thacher (and, later, others) expressed by tying a tin can was usually decisive.[4]

One of the SG's more distinctive practices is known as "confessing error." If a private attorney wins a case he thinks he should have lost in a lower federal court, he is likely to accept his victory in diplomatic silence. But when the government wins on grounds that strike the Solicitor General as unjust, he may "confess error" and recommend that the Supreme Court overturn the flawed decision. Most confessions of error involve criminal convictions, and happen for a range of reasons: a jury was selected unfairly; a judge gave faulty instructions to the jury before asking its members to reach a verdict; there was scant evidence supporting the verdict.

Confessions of error please almost no one but the SG and the defendant, who goes free. The government lawyers who have tried the case feel betrayed. The judge whose decision the SG wants overturned thinks the rug has been pulled out from under him by a double-dealing government. Judge Learned Hand sometimes complained, "It's bad enough to have the Supreme Court reverse you, but I will be damned if I will be reversed by some Solicitor General."[5] Some current members of the Supreme Court—Chief Justice Rehnquist and Justice Byron White, in particular—clearly dislike the practice, and browbeat the SG when he steps up to confess.[6] Rehnquist has urged his colleagues that they should not "respond in Pavlovian fashion"[7] when the SG confesses error, but should instead make their own ruling on the case.

But Archibald Cox, who was SG from 1961 to 1965 and who ranks with Davis and former Supreme Court Justice Robert Jackson as one of the three most respected Solicitors, has expressed a stalwart's faith in the practice of confessing error. "It tests the strength of our belief that the office has a peculiar responsibility to the Court," he told the Chicago Bar Association in 1962, during his tenure as Solicitor.[8] "It affects the way all our other cases are presented. If we are willing to take a somewhat disinterested and wholly candid position even when it means surrendering a victory, then all our other cases will be presented with a greater degree of restraint, with a greater degree of candor, and with a longer view, perhaps, than otherwise." The view expressed by Cox was originally endorsed in 1942 by the Supreme Court, in an opinion that declared, "The public trust reposed in the law enforcement officers of the Government requires that they be quick to confess error when, in their opinion, a miscarriage of justice may result from their remaining silent."[9]

The best-known instance of a Solicitor General acting with candor and disinterest, to use Cox's terms, occurred in 1955, when Senator Joseph McCarthy was just past his heyday and the influence of McCarthyism was still heavy. Someone accused John Peters, a physician, of disloyalty to the United States and membership in the Communist Party. Peters was a senior professor of medicine at Yale University, and had advised the Surgeon General for years as a consultant. The government found Peters innocent of the charges in eight separate hearings held over four years, but he was eventually judged unfit for government service by an agency known as the Loyalty Review Board.[10] The board relied on confidential informers and would not let Peters know the identities of, or cross-examine, these witnesses. He claimed he had a constitutional right to confront them and to rebut the charges they made against him. At every stage of the board's hearings against him, the only evidence publicly introduced was favorable testimony from an ex-president of Yale, a distinguished federal judge, and others in the doctor's corner. The case against him was based on secret testimony—as the chairman of the review board put it, on "evidence given by confidential informants not disclosed" to Peters.[11]

The Solicitor General was Simon Sobeloff, who held the post from 1954 to 1956. When Peters appealed, Sobeloff concluded that it would do no one any good for the Justice Department to oppose him in the Supreme Court. With the encouragement of Attorney General Herbert Brownell, Jr.,[12] the SG set out narrow grounds for siding with the doctor. As Sobeloff indicated, the case had "far-reaching importance."[13] It was bad for Peters to be kept in the dark about his accusers, but it was worse that the members of the Loyalty Review Board, acting as judges, were also ignorant about the identities and, therefore, the reliability of some of the informants. The SG called this "well-nigh indefensible," and concluded, "The President recently said in his State of the Union Message: 'We shall continue to ferret out and to destroy communist subversion. We shall, in the process, carefully preserve our traditions and the basic rights of every American citizen.' Now is the time, and this case the appropriate occasion, I believe, for showing the country that the Administration is as firmly pledged to the second sentence as the first."[14]

Brownell asked other senior officials at the Justice Department to consider Sobeloff's argument. FBI Director J. Edgar Hoover strongly disapproved, and Brownell rejected the Solicitor General's proposal.[15] Sobeloff decided his only option was to withhold the SG's backing from the government's case. He refused to sign the government's brief or to argue its merits before the Supreme Court, and another Justice Department official took over the case. The Court ruled against the government and for Peters, though the Justices did not address the major constitutional question.

Outside the Court's rarefied circle, the idea of refusing to represent the government may sound like the gesture of a prima donna.
If you do not like what the government stands for, why not quit?
The answer lies in the SG's responsibility to the Court as well as
the Executive, and, because of that, Soboloff's decision set a standard of integrity for SGs to come. It also cost him considerably.
Prior to Soboloff's taking his stand, he had been promised a seat
on the Court of Appeals for the District of Columbia, perhaps as
a step to the Supreme Court. ("Every time Soboloff comes to see
me," said Justice Felix Frankfurter, "I feel as if he's taking my
temperature.")[16] Not long afterward, a seat on the appeals court
came open, but Soboloff was passed over in favor of the man who
had taken on the Peters case for the government—Warren Burger.
Burger made his name as a conservative foil to the liberal majority
of the D.C. Circuit, and later was appointed Chief Justice of the
United States. Soboloff eventually filled a seat on the federal Court
of Appeals in Maryland.

Had Soboloff gone on to the Supreme Court, he would have
been one of a handful of SGs who have subsequently won such
appointment. They include William Howard Taft, Stanley Reed,
Robert Jackson, and Thurgood Marshall. Lloyd Wheaton Bowers
would have been in this group, but he died before President Taft
was able to appoint him.[17] With such other distinguished figures
as Archibald Cox, the first Watergate Special Prosecutor, the SGs-
turned-Justices lead a pantheon of highly respected lawyers who
have served in the SG's office and gone on to positions of wide
esteem in the law. Many of the more prominent former SGs may
have become judges in part because the SG's office itself has a
judicial cast.[18] A young law professor who hopes to work there
said, "It's the only spot, besides a judgeship, where your job is to
figure out what *you* think is the right answer for the law and then
to present your argument to the highest court in the land."[19]

The post itself gets a lot of deference from members of the bar,
whatever their station. In 1940, Frank Murphy, an experienced and
vain politician then freshly appointed to the Supreme Court, asked
a clerk if any member of that bench had ever held as many important public offices as Murphy himself. "Well, there was Taft," the
clerk answered. "He was Solicitor General, he was a Circuit Court

judge, he was president of the Philippines Commission, he was Secretary of War, he was President of the United States, and, of course, he was Chief Justice." Crestfallen, the new Justice asked, "He was Solicitor General, too?"[20]

Not all the stories about the SG's office make dignified heroes of their subject. From 1933 to 1935, a North Carolina trial lawyer named J. Crawford Biggs was Solicitor. One Justice referred to him as "Serjeant Buzfuz," after the Dickens character whom Biggs seemed to resemble.[21] In the eyes of an attorney who worked for him in the SG's office, Biggs was "kindly, honest, and gentle, and just unqualified for the job."[22] After the new man's first Term as SG, the Justices sent word to President Roosevelt that Biggs should be forbidden to argue again if the Administration wanted to win any cases before the Court.[23]

Part of the blame for Biggs's appointment can be laid on Felix Frankfurter. Then a professor at Harvard Law School, he had declined Franklin Roosevelt's offer of the post. "I was lunching with Mr. Justice Holmes on March 8, 1933, the occasion of his ninety-second birthday," Frankfurter wrote in a memo to himself,[24] when he was summoned to see the President. "I want you to be Solicitor General," Roosevelt told him. "This took me completely off my feet," Frankfurter reported, but he apparently recovered quickly. "If you don't mind my saying so," he told the President, "I think I know the demands of that office perhaps more completely than there is reason for you knowing them. I have known about the work of that office almost from the time that I left the Law School. It is exciting and profoundly important professional work. But if a man is to be Solicitor General, he must make up his mind that it will absorb sixteen hours of the day." Frankfurter added, "It is my genuine conviction—I am sure it is so—that I can do more to be of use to you by staying in Cambridge than by becoming Solicitor General."

After Frankfurter convinced Roosevelt he could serve the New Deal better from Harvard than from the Justice Department ("Felix is a stubborn pig!" FDR grumbled,[25] but the President did not hold it against Frankfurter, and eventually appointed him to the Supreme Court), the professor suggested that Roosevelt name Dean Acheson instead. Acheson was a partner in a leading Wash-

ington law firm now known as Covington & Burling and a former
law clerk to Justice Holmes. As one former Solicitor put it, "He
was well qualified, would have been a fine SG, and would doubt-
less have gone on to the Supreme Court." [26] But Roosevelt could
not appoint him: Acheson's father was Episcopal Bishop of Con-
necticut, and had refused to grant a divorce to Homer Cummings,
blocking Cummings from a third marriage in the church. Cummings was by then Roosevelt's Attorney General, and he vetoed
Acheson. Roosevelt threw up his hands and said, "Well, get me
somebody!" [27] And in place of Acheson, who later became a distinguished Secretary of State, Cummings and the President chose J.
Crawford Biggs.

Biggs was not the only ill-chosen SG. J. Howard McGrath, the
Solicitor from 1945 to 1946, distinguished himself by leaving his
duties almost completely to his assistants. [28] He had been appointed
for political reasons, [29] and he was the only SG to argue no cases
at all before the Supreme Court while he held the title. [30] He was
elevated to Attorney General after a year as Solicitor, but he fell
into shady dealings, and was charged with covering up the abuses
of some cronies. He resigned. [31]

Walter Cummings, Jr. (no relation to Homer), [32] also became
Solicitor General for reasons besides pure merit. His tenure officially began in December 1952, in Harry Truman's last full month
as President, and it lasted ninety days, until soon after Dwight
Eisenhower was sworn in—the shortest stint ever for an SG. In
the SG's office and at the Supreme Court, the thirty-six-year-old
Cummings was known as the "boy wonder." The word was he
had been brought back from private practice to become Solicitor
(he had already spent six years as an assistant to the SG) because
his father, the chairman of a big Chicago bank, had guaranteed
some loans for Truman's 1948 campaign. [33] ("That's the first I've
heard of it," Cummings said when he was asked about this.) Whatever the story, Cummings later proved himself. After practicing
law for the next decade, he was appointed to the U.S. Court of
Appeals for the Seventh Circuit, in Chicago, where he now sits
regularly on a three-judge panel composed entirely of alumni from
the SG's office.

Because of the stellar quality of his aides, boasted Francis Biddle, who was Solicitor in 1940 and 1941, "My assistants could draw

rings around most of their contemporaries in private practice." He went on, "The Solicitor General's office was small, compact, and easily managed, with a tradition that excluded hacks and enlisted men of marked ability, all of them young." [34] Biddle and others relied on gifted lawyers, some of whom backed up three, four, or five SGs, and then moved on to more visible assignments. Not long before Biddle's time, when Stanley Reed was Solicitor General (from 1935 to 1938), the assistants included perhaps the most talented lawyers who ever worked in the office. Among them were Edward Ennis, who became head of the American Civil Liberties Union; Warner Gardner, later a well-regarded Washington lawyer at his firm of Shea & Gardner; Henry Hart, who earned a reputation as a pioneering scholar for his inquiries into federal law and the legal process; Alger Hiss, the central figure in a perjury trial of the nineteen-fifties, before his rise and fall; Charles Horsky, eventually a senior partner at Covington & Burling; Harold Leventhal, later an influential member of the U.S. Court of Appeals for the District of Columbia; and Charles Wyzanski, who made his mark as a strong-willed federal trial judge in Boston.

Onetime lawyers in the SG's office tend to be proud and even sentimental about their service, showing off the collections of quill pens they have picked up from counsel's table at their arguments in the Supreme Court. (Before every argument at the Court, a bailiff lays out on both counsels' tables writing quills like the ones originally used by Chief Justice John Marshall, and lawyers are welcome to take them as souvenirs.) [35] Though his former aides sometimes confess that Reed was the only SG to faint before the Supreme Court in the middle of one of his own arguments, [36] they treasure a picture of the Reed gang of assistants, decked out in double-breasted suits with formal vests, as a prized keepsake.

Biggs was firmly propped up by Erwin Griswold, and McGrath by Paul Freund, a former law clerk to Justice Louis Brandeis and aide to Reed. Both Griswold and Freund confirmed their youthful promise by later accomplishments. Griswold became dean of the Harvard Law School and, after twenty-one years in charge, returned to the Justice Department as Solicitor General from 1967 to 1973, under Presidents Lyndon Johnson and Richard Nixon. Freund became a great constitutional scholar and the editor of a definitive history of the Supreme Court. Outside academic circles, he is sometimes recognized as the man who turned down President John F. Kennedy's offer of the Solicitor Generalship. Freund's work on the history of the Court had just begun when the offer came, after the election in 1960, and he felt he should not abandon his new venture. "I'd rather make history than write it," [37] Kennedy told Freund, probably not knowing that Freund had already made some history as McGrath's stand-in.

During his time in the SG's office, Freund once made a memorable argument for the government in a minor case. By the time he was supposed to speak, the Justices had said everything he had planned to, in their harsh questions to his opposing counsel. Freund rose and said, "May it please the Court, there is a typographical error on page ten of our brief," which he corrected. "If there are no questions, the government rests." The Justices looked surprised but then pleased, and gave the United States a unanimous decision. For years afterward, Felix Frankfurter told friends about Freund's moment, "Since I've been on the Court, I've heard learned arguments, I've heard powerful arguments, I've heard eloquent arguments. But I've heard only one *perfect* argument." [38]

The aide who guided the SG's office while Walter Cummings carried the title was Robert Stern. He never became as well known as Griswold or Freund, even in legal circles, but he may have achieved as much influence. There are many books written by former Solicitors or by lawyers on the SG's staff ("This manuscript was originally written in odd intervals between arguments in Court as Solicitor General," Robert Jackson wrote in the introduction to his book *The Struggle for Judicial Supremacy*), [39] and not all are good. James Beck (SG from 1921 to 1925) was a reactionary man, whose trademark in oral argument before the Supreme Court was quoting liberally from Shakespeare. ("I hope to God Mrs. Beck likes Shakespeare!" Justice Holmes muttered at the close of one of Beck's arguments, loudly enough for many in the courtroom to hear.) [40] Beck also wrote a primer called *The Constitution of the United States*, which a leading constitutional scholar of the time, Thomas Reed Powell, mocked in the *New Republic*. "The new book which Mr. Beck has written about the Constitution is a very different kind of book," he observed. "You can read it without thinking." [41]

In 1950, Stern co-authored with Eugene Gressman, professor

of law at the University of North Carolina, a book titled *Supreme Court Practice,* which answered a need of many attorneys—and of the Court. Now in its sixth edition, and co-authored as well by a former Deputy Solicitor General named Stephen M. Shapiro, the tome (1,030 pages long, and sold for ninety-five dollars in 1986) is accurately billed as offering "everything that a lawyer should want to know in prosecuting or defending a case in the Supreme Court."[42] On its endpapers the volume includes floor plans of the Supreme Court building, so lawyers who use the book can find their way from the checkroom or the lawyers' lounge on the first floor to the Clerk's office and the cafeteria on the floor below, or to the Library on the third floor. Since the book was first published, the Justices have sometimes taken suggestions for changes in the Court's procedures that are made in one edition and adopted them as official rules reported in the next.[43]

Erwin Griswold is now the patriarch of the extended SG family. His memory of office lore stretches back to 1929, when, at the age of twenty-five, he first joined the four other lawyers then on staff, and it covers almost half the history of the Solicitor General. Many other lawyers, who once worked there or still do, have memories that help define the SG's tradition as well. "If there is a secret handshake," said David Strauss, a former assistant to the Solicitor General and now an assistant professor at the University of Chicago Law School, "it is that there is a way of being a good government lawyer, with the government's interests in mind. There is a feeling of unity, and it's never stronger than when you know you have differences of opinion about policy, but are bound in your commitment to keep the barbarians at bay, to maintain the integrity of the law."[44] Solicitor General Frederick Lehmann once declared in a brief confessing error for the government, "The United States wins its point whenever justice is done its citizens in the courts." His declaration was carved into the rotunda of the Attorney General's office at the Department of Justice as a reminder to all his visitors, and it is a motto of the SG.[45]

In the terms of the Solicitor's office, it has been important for the SG to be "independent" in order to fulfill his duty to both the Executive Branch and the Supreme Court, and to help the courts do justice. Former SG Francis Biddle crystallized the theory of independence in his memoir titled *In Brief Authority.*[46] The SG, he wrote, "is responsible neither to the man who appointed him"—that is, the President—"nor to his immediate superior in the hierarchy of administration"—the Attorney General. "The total responsibility is his, and his guide is only the ethic of his law profession framed in the ambience of his experience and judgment. And he represents the most powerful client in the world. Nor are there any of the drawbacks that usually go with public work, no political compromises, no shifts and substitutes, no cunning deviations, no considerations of expediency," Biddle wrote. "The Solicitor General has no master to serve except his country."

Biddle's words describe an ideal that has never been entirely fulfilled. Not even he questioned that the Solicitor General works for the Attorney General and serves at the pleasure of the President.[47] He understood that the word "independent" does not mean the SG should be free to argue points of view that regularly diverge from the administration's. The Executive Branch is in some sense the SG's client, and within the bounds of the law the SG must strive to represent its interests as they change from one administration to the next. In any case, he is not likely to disagree often or by much, because a President will not appoint—and certainly will not keep—a Solicitor who does not share his vision of the law.

Nonetheless, by tradition, and because of his responsibilities to the Court, an SG must be free to reach his own carefully reasoned conclusions about the proper answer to a question of law, without second-guessing or insistence that his legal advice regularly conform to the politics of the administration he represents. An SG must have the independence to exercise his craft as a lawyer on behalf of the institution of government, without being a mouthpiece for the President. To a remarkable degree, as each Solicitor General has placed his own stamp on the job, he and his staff have often made arguments to the Supreme Court as if they had no greater authority to satisfy within the government than the SG himself and the traditions of the office. The government has profited from this standard, and, according to lawyers who represent the government and those who regularly oppose it, so has the rest of the country.[48]

III

The SG and
the Supreme Court

THE RELATIONSHIP BETWEEN the Supreme Court and
the SG's office has long been more intimate than anyone at either
place likes to acknowledge. From the nineteen-twenties, and possi-
bly before, through the early seventies, once a Solicitor General
was confirmed by the Senate, he began his tenure by paying his
respects to the Court and formally calling on each of the Justices.[1]
As an old SG hand put it, "They impressed on the Solicitor
General their reliance on the accuracy and trustworthiness of the
government's briefs, and their expectation of high quality. They
put the fear of the Lord in a new SG, and he would come back
to the office determined that the highest standards would be met."[2]
During the first visit of one new SG, Justice Frankfurter gave him
detailed instructions to pass on to the lawyers in the SG's office:
one should keep his voice up during arguments, another shouldn't
talk so much, and a third was hopelessly dull and should not be
allowed to argue at all. Paul Freund said, "It doesn't take a sledge-
hammer to make an impression when a member of the Court says
something to the Solicitor General."

The Justices also, then and now, have kept up with the lawyers
in the SG's office while they are on active duty. In 1985, one Justice
told about attending lunches with the assistants and the deputies,
though not with the SG himself, and laughed, adding, "That
should make the hair stand up on the backs of the necks of private
attorneys when they hear about it."[3] He explained, "The first time
I was asked to go, I raised the invitation with one of my colleagues.
'Anything wrong with this?' I said. 'Hell, no!' he told me. 'It's
been going on for years.' I know the private bar may wonder about

the propriety of this sort of lunch, but if they don't have confidence in us, I don't know what to say." After the Justice spoke, a deputy in the SG's office was asked, "When was the last time you had lunch with a Supreme Court Justice?" He said, "Last Tuesday." [4]

During the fifties, when Felix Frankfurter was on the Supreme Court and a number of his younger friends, including a former law clerk, were in the SG's office, he began to meet regularly with the SG's lawyers. [5] The group invited other Justices to lunch as well, and since then, a few times a year, the SG's staff gets together with a Justice to sort through administrative details (whether the Court should retain its current limits on the number of pages allowed in briefs, for example) [6] and to talk. Occasionally, a Justice will give the lawyers a thought about an aspect of their duties before the Court that spurs them to try doing better at it. Justice Rehnquist once told the group that even a terrible oral argument was useful to the Justices, because it was the one event requiring all nine members of the bench to focus on a case at the same time. He sent back some lawyers thinking that they should prepare more conscientiously for oral arguments. [7]

The unusual private ties between the Supreme Court and the SG's office are matched by their close public dealings. Whenever a member of the Court dies, the SG is asked to call a meeting of the Supreme Court bar to honor the Justice. [8] Lawyers in the SG's office say this duty makes the Solicitor the president of the Court bar. [9] (He isn't, because there is no such post.) [10] The Justices also call on former Solicitors for help in special Court projects. Until the late thirties, for instance, there was no uniform code of civil procedure for use in federal courts; in the absence of common guidelines, each federal court used the rules of the state where it sat. This practice yielded a disarray of rulings by federal judges, and half the appeals in the federal courts were about the weblike details of procedure. Chief Justice Charles Evans Hughes appointed a commission headed by ex-SG William Mitchell to devise some uniform rules, and the Justices accepted eighty-six of the group's eighty-eight recommendations. [11]

The Justices also give the SG special dispensations in Court. In the Supreme Court's rules, the Solicitor is one of the few lawyers allowed to file a brief as a friend of the Court without the permission of the parties to the suit.[12] The SG is also the only amicus regularly given time to argue his case before the Court. Unless he abuses the privilege, the SG is the sole advocate to whom the Justices regularly grant requests for extensions of time to file papers with the Court.[13] The special treatment for the Solicitor is most visible to outsiders in the SG's briefs themselves. Until 1980, the Court allowed private law firms to pick their own colors for the covers of their briefs, and attorneys worked hard to distinguish themselves in the minds of the Justices by the colors they chose. (In a case about fishing rights, the Puget Sound Gillnetters Association filed briefs in salmon pink.) The rules of the Court now assign the colors that lawyers are supposed to use for covers of documents submitted to the Justices, according to the document's role in a case: petitions for writs of certiorari must be white; responses to petitions light orange; appellants' briefs on the merits light blue. One exception to the new rule was permitted: the SG's filings, and no other party's, were to be bound in gray, regardless of the government's role in the case. The exception was a concession to the SG's office, which had filed briefs clad in gray for so long that the government's submissions are still called gray briefs. But some years before the SG's office had switched to tan. The messenger service that runs twice a day between the Justice Department and the Supreme Court carries only tan-covered filings from the SG's office.[14]

Stern, Gressman, and Shapiro's *Supreme Court Practice* explains most of the Court's procedures, including the ones that favor the SG, but there is a practice engaged in by almost no one but the SG's office that the book doesn't mention. It's called "lodging," which is not a standard procedure. At the office of the Clerk of the Supreme Court, it is generally used to refer to the ordinary practitioners' technique of dropping off at the Court certain materials that are part of the record in a case coming up for review. The documents would reach the Court soon enough through regular channels, but on the chance the Justices or their law clerks want to start studying the case right away, one of the parties lodges the papers (e.g., part of the trial transcript or a key piece of evidence) with the Clerk.[15]

For the SG's office, lodging means something different: a case runs through a trial and an appeal, and it arrives at the Supreme Court; the SG's team considers the merits of the case, and finds a document (an annual report from Congress, a study from a government agency) that, while not in the trial record, sheds light on the government's argument; the SG's lawyers "lodge" the goods with the Clerk (they do it one or two dozen times a year) [16] and inform the Justices that the materials are there in case they want to examine the papers. This runs contrary to the rule that appeals courts cannot consider evidence that has not been presented to the trial court below.

A deputy clerk who was asked which Supreme Court rule permits lodging replied, "There is no rule. It's just a practice." [17] He went on, "Any lawyer can lodge documents with the Court, as long as the material qualifies as the kind of background the Justices could take judicial notice of and refer to in their opinions as generally known facts." But only the SG's office regularly lodges papers that are not part of the record. Most lawyers don't know about the practice, because it's not in the Court's rules. And, as one former assistant to the SG put it, "It rarely happens that private lawyers lodge material; they've usually been with the case a long time and have already brought forth their best stuff." [18] The SG's office, by contrast, always takes a fresh look at a case. "The truth," the ex-assistant went on, "is that the time the SG's office has to review cases when they are in the lower courts is minuscule. Until we get to the nitty-gritty of preparing a Supreme Court argument, we don't give it our best. But then we do." A Deputy Solicitor added, "We're not entitled to make a new argument in the Supreme Court, but if we think of a way to make the old argument better, we sure try." [19]

In 1975, Solicitor General Robert Bork was planning to file an amicus brief supporting the death penalty in a case pending before the Court. [20] One of the arguments raised by opponents of the death penalty is that it does not deter criminals, so it cannot fulfill a basic function of criminal law. The lawyers in the SG's office who were working on the case didn't have much besides logic on which to rely in their rebuttal of this claim, but late one night the deputy in charge was unwinding in front of his TV, and he caught the end of a debate about the death penalty on a talk show. [21] One of the participants mentioned an unpublished study by Isaac Ehrlich, an economist at the University of Chicago, which went a step beyond any of the well-known work in the field. [22] Ehrlich claimed that each additional execution of a convicted murderer might save eight lives, because that many potential offenders would be deterred from committing murder. The deputy tracked down Ehrlich and asked if he could see the study (it was called "The Deterrent Effect of Capital Punishment: A Question of Life and Death") for possible use in the SG's brief. The SG lodged the study with the Supreme Court.

One lawyer opposing the SG's office in the death-penalty case was David Kendall, now a partner in the Washington law firm of Williams & Connolly. When the SG's office called him to report about the government's plan to lodge the Ehrlich study with the Supreme Court, Kendall said, "I went through the roof. It wasn't even published, it was full of arcane mathematics, and it was indigestible to the average reader. And the copy they lodged was a dim Xerox. The whole business was an outrage." To Kendall, the study failed to meet the Supreme Court's standard because it did not qualify as general knowledge. Since the majority opinion of the Supreme Court did not rely on the study, however, it also appeared to have little to do with the outcome of the case. "As far as I'm concerned," Kendall said, "it was a low blow without lasting consequences." [23]

But the case nicely framed the lodging question. "This is an adversary system," Kendall said. "Just because the SG has what he thinks is the best available information doesn't mean he can put it into the record for the Supreme Court to consider. You don't have safeguards at that stage. The Supreme Court is not a trial court. Letting the other side know about new material doesn't cure the central vice. You can't cross-examine the preparer of a report lodged with the Court, so lodging ends up being a tool for the government to wrest some advantage for itself. They can ask agencies to prepare authoritative-sounding material that is not necessarily reliable and the opponent is caught on the horns of a dilemma: he doesn't want to be seen as overreacting, so he doesn't want to file a motion to strike the stuff that's been lodged with the

Court; but he doesn't have a real opportunity to respond to the substance. The result is that lodging is a subversion of the process for finding facts, and there's not much a private lawyer can do about it.

"In the Supreme Court," he went on, "the SG's office is the home team. They are always up there, and whether or not you assume they have right and truth on their side because they are the government, it's an adversary system. Both sides in the conflict compete under fair and noble rules, under which justice is done when there is the fullest airing of facts and arguments by both sides. The government is the government, and should be fully respected. The SG's office serves as a buffer between the Judiciary and the Executive Branch. But it isn't a benign and altruistic referee guiding every step of the law. Otherwise, there'd be no need for lawsuits."

Most contests in which the SG's office lodges fresh documents draw no special notice from the Supreme Court. But occasionally the Justices have broken their silence about this unorthodox procedure. In a case about drug trafficking, Justice Byron White all but thanked the SG's office in a footnote for the documents that it had lodged.[24] In 1985, Justice John Paul Stevens got off what lawyers in the SG's office considered a barbed footnote about lodging. Writing for his colleagues in a majority opinion, Stevens held for the SG in a case about a cutback in food stamps, but he did not like the government's use of little-known facts to shore up its argument.[25] Another Justice said, "Some years ago, we had a case about avocadoes up here, in which the question was whether a California statute setting the amount of oil in an avocado was superseded by a federal law. The record was meager, so I sent my law clerk down to the Agriculture Department to find some stuff. Our feeling was it's not so important what facts you use to decide it as what principle you rely on, but you should gather the best information that you can. The SG knows this and argues that if the Court thinks this way, why shouldn't the SG? That's the sort of thing that sometimes causes eyes to pop."[26]

Lodging and other practices that favor the Solicitor General point up the exceptional terms that sometimes govern dealings between the Supreme Court and the SG's office: the Solicitor

General plays by different rules because he represents the United States. If the SG's office owes a special duty to the Court, and the Justices hold the SG's lawyers to a higher standard of craft, why shouldn't the Court give those lawyers some extra scope?

The most amazing episode of intimacy between the SG's office and the Supreme Court took place in the early fifties.[27] An assistant named Philip Elman was in charge of civil-rights cases for the office through the reigns of five SGs. He was later appointed a member of the Federal Trade Commission, and was for many years a professor at the Georgetown University Law Center. "It may sound sentimental and corny in these very cynical days," he recalled in 1983 for Columbia University's Oral History Project, "but we took it for granted, without making any big fuss over it or being self-righteous, that our job was to do justice, to treat people fairly and not give a damn what anyone thought." Elman helped formulate the government's position and write its amicus brief in a landmark case in which the Supreme Court struck down restrictions that prevented blacks from buying property, and he wrote other briefs calling for desegregation of dining cars on trains, of law schools, and of graduate schools. When it came to asking the Supreme Court to outlaw segregation in public schools, Solicitor General Philip Perlman drew the line. He would not let the government argue that an 1896 case called Plessy v. Ferguson,[28] upholding the doctrine of separate-but-equal, should be overturned.

Like other assistants who worked for the SG during and after the New Deal, Elman joined the office with the encouragement of Felix Frankfurter. In the days when Justices had only one clerk (most Justices now hire four), Elman had been Frankfurter's. As Elman told the story, the two became close friends, and the Justice influenced his former aide's view of history. "The entire length of our relationship from 1941 to 1965, when he died," Elman said, "the Justice and I would talk on the phone a good deal. He would call me almost every Sunday night at home. He would have gone through the Sunday papers, and after dinner he liked to talk, or 'schmooze,' as he would say. We'd have a long, relaxed, gossipy conversation for an hour and a half sometimes." With "certain unspoken restrictions," according to Elman ("we never discussed a case that I had argued"), they seemed to talk about almost everything. Frankfurter's colleagues (he referred to them in code—Robert Jackson, for example, was Jamestown, the town in upstate New York he came from, and Stanley Reed was the "chamer," meaning "ass" or "fool" in Yiddish) were a favorite topic.

"And along came the first of the kind of miracles that Frankfurter was waiting for," Elman reported. J. Howard McGrath, who had moved from the SG's quarters to the Attorney General's during the Truman Administration, and was Perlman's boss, resigned after he was accused of corruption. President Truman replaced him with a former congressman and federal judge named James McGranery. "McGranery, to put it as simply as I can," Elman recalled, "was a kind of nut." McGranery and Perlman didn't get along, and the Solicitor General quit as soon as he could. Robert Stern became Acting SG, and he and Elman went to see the new Attorney General. Elman: "We told McGranery, who hated Perlman, who had been very happy to see him go, that Perlman, even though the Department had consistently taken the position that Plessy was wrong and should be overruled, had refused to participate as amicus in the pending school segregation cases. We told him the Department of Justice should stick to its position and file an amicus brief in the Court. McGranery's immediate response was, 'You're right, boys. Go ahead and write a brief.'

"So that's how we happened to file the first brief in Brown v. Board of Education in December 1952, signed by McGranery as Attorney General and by me. . . . We were the first to suggest . . . that if the Court should hold that racial segregation in schools is unconstitutional, it should give district courts a reasonable period of time to work out the details and timing of implementation of the decision. In other words, 'with all deliberate speed.' " For Elman, "This first brief we filed in December 1952 is the one thing I'm proudest of in my whole career."

The Supreme Court's embrace of the "deliberate speed" formula is often criticized on the ground that it gave Southern states an excuse for avoiding compliance with the Court's ruling. But, according to Elman, the government would not have filed a brief without this formula, and the government's participation in the first Brown case was crucial, because it signaled to the Justices that the Executive Branch was ready to enforce a call for desegregation of public schools. Elman has commented about this proposal that "it was entirely unprincipled, it was just plain wrong as a matter of constitutional law, to suggest that someone whose personal constitutional rights were being violated should be denied relief." And yet, in his view, it became a rallying point for the Supreme Court, a notion that ultimately helped the Justices reach a unanimous decision.

Where did this idea come from? "Not from Frankfurter," Elman says, before seeming to contradict himself: "But it did grow out of my many conversations with him over a period of many months. He told me what he thought, what the other Justices were telling him they thought. I knew from him what their positions were. If the issue was inescapably presented in yes-or-no terms, he could not count five votes on the Court to overrule Plessy." Hugo Black, for example, the former Alabama senator who was counted as a vote to overturn the precedent, warned his colleagues what the change would mean. "The Klan is going to ride again," he prophesied. "This will be the end of liberalism in the South."

The Supreme Court heard arguments on Brown during the 1952 Term, but could not reach a decision. "There's no question that the grand strategist in all this inside the Court was F.F.," Elman has said of Frankfurter. "He was writing memos to his colleagues and having his clerk, Alex Bickel"—who later became a renowned professor at Yale Law School—"do research into the legislative history of the Fourteenth Amendment, the results of which he then circulated to the Court. To use the Yiddish word that Frankfurter used all the time, he was the *Kochleffel*. It means cooking spoon, stirring things up; the man stirring everything up inside the Court was Frankfurter. They couldn't decide the cases, they didn't know what to do with them, they had no majority, and they hadn't even taken a formal vote, because they didn't want to harden anybody's position. So in the summer of 1953 before they adjourned, they set the cases down for reargument: they asked five questions of the parties, and they invited the Attorney General of the United States and the attorneys general of all the states requiring or authorizing segregation to file briefs and present oral argument."

McGranery had by then been replaced by Herbert Brownell,

Jr., as Attorney General. After the Supreme Court's order for reargument, Brownell called a meeting to decide how the government should respond to the Court's invitation. Elman and Robert Stern, as Acting SG, considered the invitation "the equivalent of a royal command," as it would be today. But others among the AG's advisers (including Warren Burger) said that Brownell was free to accept or refuse the offer, and recommended that he stand clear of a case which was certain to set off tremors in the South. Brownell's opening move was to shift responsibility for the case from the SG's office to his own, and ask J. Lee Rankin to oversee the project.

"Some time later," Elman has said, "I think much later—I remember writing a letter to Frankfurter during the summer telling him that nothing, absolutely nothing, was going on in the Department of Justice—Rankin called me into his office and said that he had gotten the green light from Brownell. I'm sure Brownell had talked to Eisenhower about it. The feeling we all had at the time was that Eisenhower would not be sympathetic to the idea, because he was known to believe that public education was something for the states, the federal government should stay out of it, and this problem was the Court's and not his as President. So I give Brownell and Rankin the most credit for the Eisenhower Administration's decision to participate."

Elman was relieved of his other duties in the SG's office, and put in charge of writing the government's brief. When he finished, Rankin read it and made no changes. Over a period of weeks, when he had free time, Brownell called Elman in, and the assistant and the Attorney General went over the brief. They "would sit there and he would read it," Elman said, "and if there was something he didn't understand or agree with, he would stop and ask me to explain, or justify it. We did a little rewriting in his office."

At the close of the summer, before the government filed its brief, Chief Justice Fred Vinson died. He was a onetime senator from Kentucky whose reluctance to confront the issue raised in Brown was well known. When Frankfurter had tabulated votes for and against overturning Plessy, Vinson's was one the Justice marked as a no. As Elman tells it, "Frankfurter was then in New England where he spent the summer. The Justices all came back to Washington to attend the funeral services. I met Frankfurter, I think at Union Station, and he was in high spirits. I shouldn't really report all this, but this is history and, as he used to say, history has its claims."

Elman: "Frankfurter said to me, 'I'm in mourning,' sarcastically. What he meant was that Vinson's departure from the Court was going to remove the roadblock in Brown. As long as Vinson was Chief Justice, they could never get unanimity or anything close to it. If Vinson dissented, Reed would surely join him, Tom Clark probably would too, and Jackson would write that the issue should be left to Congress. Anyway, Frankfurter happily said to me, 'I'm in mourning.' And, with that viselike grip of his, he grabbed me by the arm and, looking me straight in the eye, said, 'Phil, this is the first solid piece of evidence I've ever had that there really is a God.' "

Although it was never publicly announced, Earl Warren had been slated to become Solicitor General until Vinson died. [29] Instead, President Eisenhower appointed him to replace Vinson as Chief Justice and, in December 1953, Brown v. Board of Education was reargued. Among the lawyers who presented views for or against overruling Plessy v. Ferguson were three Solicitors General, though none was then in office. [30] John W. Davis, at the age of eighty, and three and a half decades past his tenure as SG, made an emotional speech on behalf of separate-but-equal education that brought tears to his own eyes (and, because it endorsed segregation, also tarnished his reputation). [31] Thurgood Marshall, more than a decade before his time as Solicitor, presented part of the NAACP Legal Defense Fund's argument. J. Lee Rankin argued for the government. Though Rankin went on to do his share of advocacy when he became SG two and a half years later, the argument in Brown was his first before the Justices.

In his oral history, Philip Elman spells out his running debate with Felix Frankfurter about the most convincing argument for the government to make on the merits of the Brown case. He was also asked what he thought about possible charges that these discussions with the Justice were improper—that, at a minimum, they gave the government an unfair advantage because opposing lawyers could not rebut Elman's presentation to the Justice.

(While concurring in the view that Elman had exaggerated "both his own role and the Court's reliance on his arguments," a *New York Times* editorial called the Elman-Frankfurter collaboration "deeply disturbing" and "unethical.")[32] To put the question in perspective, imagine the uproar if word got out that, of the two dissenters in the Court's landmark decision on abortion, Roe v. Wade[33]—Justice (now Chief Justice) William Rehnquist and Justice Byron White—one had held regular conversations with one of his ex-law clerks working in the SG's office about a case dealing with that issue.

"Yes," Elman has observed, "I suppose there's a point there. I don't have any easy, snappy response to that. In Brown, I didn't consider myself a lawyer for a litigant. I considered it a cause that transcended ordinary notions about propriety in a litigation. This was not a litigation in the usual sense. I don't defend my discussions with Frankfurter; I just did what I thought was right, and I'm sure he didn't give it much thought. I regarded myself, in the literal sense, as an amicus curiae." He added, "Brown v. Board of Education, which we fully discussed, was an extraordinary case, and the ordinary rules didn't apply. In that case I knew everything, or at least he gave me the impression that I knew everything, that was going on at the Court. He told me about what was said in conference and who said it. The constitutional issue went to the heart of what kind of country we are, what kind of Constitution and Supreme Court we have: whether, almost a century after the Fourteenth Amendment was adopted, the Court could find the wisdom and courage to hold that the amendment meant what it said, that black people could no longer be singled out and treated differently because of their color, that in everything it did, government had to be color-blind.

"As I look back now, I can see myself in Brown v. Board of Education as having been his junior partner, or law clerk emeritus, in helping him work out the best solution for the toughest problem to come before the Court in this century."

In May of 1954, in a unanimous decision, the Supreme Court outlawed segregation in public schools.[34] The Justices retained jurisdiction of the case to decide how their order should be implemented, and the government's separate brief on this question contained a detail that emphasized how unusual the case really was. The government again offered the Elman "deliberate-speed" proposal: the timetable for desegregation should be flexible, and, rather than the Supreme Court, the district courts should oversee the process because they were closer to local conditions which might dictate a faster or slower pace. "It must be recognized that racial segregation in public schools is not a separate and distinct phenomenon," the draft brief lectured. "The Court's decision in these cases has outlawed a social institution which has existed for a long time in many areas throughout the country. . . ."

At this point in the final brief, there was an extraordinary addition. In a small, wiry hand, Dwight Eisenhower filled the margin and top of the galleys for the draft with a long comment to bolster an already strong expression of concern about the decision to abandon the separate-but-equal doctrine in favor of equal opportunity and integration of the races. It was wholly unprecedented for a Solicitor General to bring the proofs of any brief to a President for approval. Elman recounted, "I punctuated and put his language in more readable form. These are Eisenhower's sentences, edited by me. Where I wrote that the Court had outlawed a social institution that had existed for a long time in many areas throughout the country, he added this language (as cleaned up by me): '[Segregation is] an institution, it may be noted, which during its existence not only has had the sanction of decisions of this Court but has been fervently supported by great numbers of people as justifiable on legal and moral grounds. The Court's holding in the present cases that segregation is a denial of constitutional rights involved an express recognition of the importance of psychological and emotional factors; the impact of segregation upon children, the Court found, can so affect their entire lives as to preclude their full enjoyment of constitutional rights. In similar fashion, psychological and emotional factors are involved—and must be met with understanding and good will—in the alterations that must now take place in order to bring about compliance with the Court's decision.'[35]

"As I look at it now, thirty years later," Elman said, "I'm astonished at the liberties that I, a young lawyer in the Solicitor General's office, felt free to take with the language of the President of the United States, which he wasn't going to have an opportunity to change, because it went from me to the printer. It shows the degree of what seems to me now astonishing self-confidence, or even arrogance, I had at the time. Anyway, it was the first and only instance I know of in which the President of the United States was coauthor of a brief in the Supreme Court. I think the point he made was a valid one. I wish I had thought of it first."

IV

"Independence"

T H E T I E S B E T W E E N the Solicitor General and the Supreme Court confound the textbook notion of checks and balances exercised by each branch of government on the others, but the question of the SG's independence within the Executive Branch has been a more riveting concern to lawyers in the SG's office. Solicitors in every Democratic and Republican Administration since the nineteen-sixties have pondered this question.[1] The SGs have treated "independence" as a paradox. They recognize that they serve at the pleasure of the President, and often put the word in quotation marks. Yet they have considered it a fundamental requirement of the office of Solicitor.

Erwin Griswold was a moderate Republican when he was appointed SG by a Democrat, Lyndon Johnson, in 1967. His hobby had been the SG's office since 1929, when he first went to work there. Like William Mitchell, who was widely respected as the Democratic SG for the Republican Coolidge Administration in the twenties,[2] Griswold was praised as a worthy and nonpartisan appointment. Although his style of arguing in the Supreme Court was occasionally a stubborn one ("He's like the U.S.S. Griswold," said one Justice. "Questions from us just bounce off him harmlessly as he cruises through his speech"),[3] and he upset some Democrats in the Justice Department by taking a less aggressive stance in favor of civil rights than they wished,[4] he proved to be a good, fair-minded Solicitor.

After Johnson left office, the Nixon Administration kept him on as SG. Nixon's men thought the ex-dean of Harvard Law School added a conspicuous touch of class to the Justice Department,[5] and (except for William Rehnquist, then an Assistant At-

torney General, who refused to stand on ceremony)[6] senior officials at the department always called him Dean. Griswold had a
courtly and formidable Midwestern manner, and he believed in
protocol. Recognizing that he worked for the Attorney General
and the President, he tried to keep the Republicans as happy with
his advocacy as he had the Democrats.[7] He did not fully succeed.

In 1971, the Nixon Executive Branch forced the Supreme Court
to rule on one of the great clashes between the government and
the press in American history: the Pentagon papers dispute.[8] Before the fight became a lawsuit, Griswold counseled privately that
the government should not sue a number of newspapers that had
published parts of the Defense Department's classified history of
the Vietnam War. Attorney General John Mitchell didn't ask his
opinion. After the Nixon White House decided to sue the offenders, the case rose quickly to the Supreme Court and Griswold took
charge. The brief he eventually filed angered defenders of the press
by its assertion that publication of the papers could cause "immediate and irreparable harm to the security of the United States."[9]
But, according to Sanford Ungar in *The Papers and the Papers*,
Griswold's judgments behind closed doors belied this view. Calcu-
lating that it would take him six weeks to read through the forty-
seven volumes of the Pentagon papers and make up his own mind
about the nature of their contents, Griswold called in officials from
the Defense Department and other agencies to identify for him
items in the papers that, if published, would in their view threaten
national security. He concluded that, except in about a dozen
instances, the government should stop objecting to publication of
the history, because the only harm that would come of it was
political embarrassment. The Supreme Court refused to enjoin
publication of any part of the papers.[10]

In other cases, Griswold drew a sharper line between his own
and the Administration's views about what was legal. Following
the example of Simon Sobeloff, who fifteen years earlier had
refused to argue for the government, Griswold declined in two
cases dealing with national security and the draft; he believed the
Nixon Administration was seeking more authority for the Executive Branch than the laws in question allowed. Since the Supreme
Court was not likely to rule in the government's favor, he thought
that he would diminish his credibility with the Justices if he made

the claims that the Executive Branch wanted him to press. (In 1985, when he was asked why he believed this, Griswold said, "I've dealt with the Court for fifty-odd years, so it was perfectly obvious.") [11] Griswold also presented views about civil rights that, while sometimes too moderate for the Johnson Administration, were often too liberal for Nixon's.

The last straw for Griswold may have been his role in an antitrust case, in which he bridled at a direct order from Richard Nixon. [12] The United States had brought suit against the conglomerate then known as International Telephone & Telegraph, or ITT, on the theory that one of the firm's mergers had violated federal laws. The government lost in the lower courts and the SG's office decided it should take the case to the Supreme Court, to ensure that the lower-court ruling did not become a precedent hindering other challenges to conglomerate mergers. "I think this is a very hard case," Griswold wrote in an internal memo, "but it is an important one and Antitrust wants to go ahead, and it is in the public interest, I think, that we should learn more about what the law is in this area." [13]

Richard Nixon also thought ITT was an important case. From the Oval Office, one day in the spring of 1971, with his tape system on, Nixon called Richard Kleindienst, who, as Deputy AG, was running the Justice Department. [14] "The IT and T thing—stay the hell out of it," Nixon said. "I know all the legal things, Dick, you don't have to spell out the legal—That's right. That's right. Don't file the brief. Your—my order is to drop the God damn thing. Is that clear?" Nixon may have been interested in the case because of his taste for questions of economics—conglomerate mergers were then a major business story. It was more likely that the President had given his personal attention to the lawsuit because, as Jack Anderson reported, ITT had promised to contribute $400,000 to the Republican National Committee and the Nixon Administration for the 1972 Republican Convention if the Administration would settle the suit. [15]

Minutes after Nixon phoned him, Richard Kleindienst called Griswold into his office and asked about the status of the ITT case. The SG informed the Acting Attorney General that the government had one day left before the deadline for filing its brief at the Supreme Court. Kleindienst told him to ask the Court for a month's extension, while they figured out how to persuade the President to let the Justice Department resolve the case on legal grounds.[16] Looking back fourteen years later, Griswold said, "I would have resigned if we hadn't been able to work out the differences, because it was a direct political interference, without any professional justification. But we worked everything out, and the case got settled properly."[17] (The case also contributed to Kleindienst's downfall. A year after he officially replaced John Mitchell as Attorney General in 1972, Kleindienst resigned and pleaded guilty to having perjured himself before the Senate about the ITT affair. "I was not interfered with by anybody at the White House,"[18] he had sworn before the facts came to light.)

After Richard Nixon was reelected in 1972, Nixon unilaterally announced Griswold's resignation as Solicitor General. "I was approaching sixty-nine years old," Griswold recalled in 1985, "and had been in the office for six years, and it was entirely up to him to decide what he wanted to. But Mr. Nixon decided without telling me. I heard it from a friend who had heard it over the radio. It would have been courteous if the President had at least sent me a note, or called me over to thank me, but he didn't do either of those things. I'm rather proud of the fact that the only commission I have as Solicitor General was signed by Lyndon Johnson."[19]

THE NIXON ADMINISTRATION appointed Robert Bork to replace Griswold as Solicitor General. The President and Bork agreed about the threat to the Republic posed by what Bork called the "Imperial Judiciary." Bork was concerned about the "tyranny of the minority" (of judges, among others) and the transformation of the Supreme Court into a "naked power organ."[20] Though Bork was making a name for himself in constitutional law, and held a professorship in constitutional law at Yale Law School (the same chair William Howard Taft had filled in the early years of this century),[21] he was better known as an antitrust scholar. He had attended the University of Chicago Law School during the rise of the conservative, free-market movement in economics labeled the Chicago School. Chicago was the first university to hire an economist on a law-school faculty, and Edward Levi, who was then law-school dean and later became Attorney General under

Gerald Ford, taught an antitrust course with economist Aaron Director in which they used economic theory to rebut the law's traditional antitrust doctrine. [22] Bork recalled, "A lot of us who took the antitrust course or the economics course underwent what can only be called a religious conversion. It changed our view of the entire world." [23] He made his reputation by arguing that antitrust policies meant to spur economic efficiency often did just the opposite. [24]

At the end of the first Nixon term, Bork was invited to Camp David, where the President asked him to be SG. He had caught Nixon's attention while helping the Administration devise limits to propose to Congress on busing as a tool of school desegregation. [25] "Nixon gave me a remarkably thoughtful lecture about judicial restraint," Bork said in 1985. [26] "It was a good lecture. I could have delivered a better one, but then I'd been teaching for a long time. I had met him once before, in a meeting about busing where I happened to say that the only way the government could support a piece of pending legislation was by relying on a case called Katzenbach v. Morgan, which gave the Congress broad power to define the contents of constitutional provisions. I said, 'You don't want to do that. It's corrupt constitutional law.' Nixon turned and said, 'I believe that, but I didn't know there was a constitutional law professor in the country who did.' I suppose that first meeting was where they got the idea of making me Solicitor General."

Unlike Erwin Griswold, Bork avoided political run-ins with the Nixon Administration, which was increasingly preoccupied with Watergate during his tenure as SG. Bork, who has a beard like Rasputin's and a reputation for brilliance, was appointed by President Reagan to the U.S. Court of Appeals for the District of Columbia in 1982. Before his 1987 nomination to the Supreme Court made him famous, Bork was already a name on legal trivia quizzes. He became one after Attorney General Elliot Richardson and Deputy Attorney General William Ruckelshaus resigned rather than comply with Richard Nixon's order to fire Archibald Cox as Watergate Special Prosecutor in October of 1973. [27] ("If you really are determined to get rid of Cox," Ruckelshaus told Nixon's men, "I think Bork may be your man.") [28] As the next official in line to succeed the Attorney General, Solicitor General Bork be-

lieved it was his duty to end the confrontation between Nixon
and Cox over the Watergate inquiry. If he himself were also to
resign, Bork thought, Nixon would appoint someone from outside the Justice Department as the new Attorney General, probably from the White House staff, and the department would be
crippled by a mass resignation of angry career attorneys. Since,
unlike Richardson and Ruckelshaus, Bork had made no personal
commitment not to fire Cox, he decided to carry out the President's order. He also signed a commitment to abolish the Special Prosecutor's office, and did so. The American people, however, overwhelmingly condemned the Cox firing (Western
Union delivered over 150,000 telegrams to Washington in the
two days immediately following, and many telegrams to Congress said simply, "Impeach Nixon"), and the Nixon Administration realized that it needed to defuse this response. Bork
agreed. Despite his personal belief that ongoing Watergate inquiries by the Justice Department and the U.S. Attorney in
Washington made a special prosecutor unnecessary, with the
concurrence of the White House (and perhaps at its direction)
he appointed Leon Jaworski to succeed Cox.

During the two months after Richardson's and Ruckelshaus's
departures, Bork functioned as both Attorney General and Solicitor. He relied heavily on his Deputy SGs, until William Saxbe
became Attorney General in January of 1974. When Bork focused
again on the SG's work, he regularly acted on the philosophy that
won him the job. He worked on the Supreme Court brief that
urged the Justices to permit state laws to impose the death penalty,
and in other major cases he also presented conservative views.
Living with what he called the tension between legal principle and
political expediency, Bork regularly found means to carry the
Administration's message to the Court.[29] He was a more enthusi-
astic advocate of Nixon's legal notions than Griswold had been
(and, in the process, drove away one assistant who believed that
the former Yale professor had compromised the integrity of the
SG's judgment about the law),[30] and he was equally forthright
about making arguments favored by Ford.

Bork also showed commitment to the legal standards of the
office. During his confirmation hearings for the Solicitorship, one
senator had asked whether he would argue his own highly uncon-

ventional views about antitrust law or more mainstream interpretations. [31] He promised to defer to others in the Justice Department about the government's positions, and he did. In most instances, Daniel Friedman (now a federal judge, and then a Deputy SG) decided what to argue in antitrust. [32]

In February of 1975, Bork's former teacher and longtime friend Edward Levi was appointed Attorney General. Bork consulted with Levi about cases that might cause a stir. [33] He spent days considering whether to try persuading the Supreme Court to hear a challenge to mandatory school busing in Boston after a petition for certiorari was filed by one of the parties. He believed that busing had been used as a tool of desegregation more often than the Justices had intended when they first ruled that it was legal for courts to order busing as a last resort, [34] and that the Justices ought to remind lower-court judges that busing was only one of the possible remedies for discrimination. This was the policy of the Ford Administration, but after lengthy discussions in which the President participated, the treatment of the case was left for the Justice Department to decide, and Bork was convinced by the Attorney General and others not to enter the case. [35] (The Supreme Court denied cert., and the Boston busing plan stood.) [36]

Like Erwin Griswold, who chose not to file an amicus brief in Roe v. Wade, Bork felt no need to register an opinion for the government about each major social issue. He believed the SG's job was to represent the long-term interests of the government as much as the policies of the current Administration. Sympathetic to a Republican law-and-order view of criminal law, he nonetheless confessed error in some criminal cases. Adopting a stance like Griswold's, he refused to make oral arguments in cases he considered "fatuous." Bork mocked the tradition of the SG ("Everybody talked about it as a place where the lore was very arcane and celestial music played," he said, "so I called myself Der Meister Shyster"), [37] but he accommodated himself to it. "The SG's job is the chief purely legal job in the government," he observed in 1975. "So far, in my experience, he's been quite independent." [38]

NOT LONG AFTER Wade McCree succeeded Bork as SG, in 1977, under the Carter Administration, a case came along that put the SG's independence to a severe test. Called Regents of the University of California v. Bakke,[39] it came to stand in some lawyers' minds for the proposition that, in the final analysis, it is proper for the President and his aides to intervene at will in the affairs of the SG and to dictate the government's legal positions in the Supreme Court.[40] In fact, the case helped persuade Griffin Bell, who was the first Attorney General of the Carter Administration, of the opposite.

Allan Paul Bakke was a white engineer who wanted to attend the University of California Medical School at Davis. After his interview at Davis, a faculty member called him "a well-qualified candidate for admissions whose main hardship is the unavoidable fact that he is now 33."[41] On the medical school's admissions scale, Bakke received 468 points out of a possible 500. Earlier in the year, a rating of 470 had won automatic entry. Bakke had delayed completing his application because his mother had been ill, and by the time he filed, there were few places left in the class. He was not admitted.

Bakke applied again the next year, and was again rejected, and he filed a suit in state court, protesting his rejection. The core of his complaint was that the medical school's policy of reserving sixteen of the hundred places in its entering class for blacks, American Indians, Chicanos, and Asian Americans deprived him of his right to equal protection of the law under the Fourteenth Amendment to the Constitution. At trial, Bakke won a partial victory. (The judge ruled that the medical school had violated the Constitution by establishing a quota for admissions, but did not order Davis to admit Bakke, because Bakke had not proved he would have been admitted if the special admissions program did not exist.) On appeal to the California Supreme Court, he won again. According to Justice Stanley Mosk, who wrote the court's opinion, the Davis program violated the constitutional rights of white applicants "because it afford[ed] preference on the basis of race to persons who, by the University's own standards, [were] not as qualified for the study of medicine as non-minority applicants denied admission." In dissent, Justice Matthew Tobriner wrote an opinion that was longer than the majority's. In Tobriner's mind, the main value promoted by the Fourteenth Amendment was

racial integration. The Davis program sought that end. He regret-
ted that a remedy for the "inequalities flowing from past discrimination will inevitably result in some detriment to nonminorities,"
but as long as the remedy was "adopted in good faith to promote
integration" by using a racial classification related to that goal, the
court should uphold the program. [42]

When the Bakke case rose to the United States Supreme Court,
the federal government was not a party and the Justices did not
ask the SG to submit an amicus brief giving an opinion on the law.
But the government kept watch on the case. Drew Days, who was
the first black to head the Civil Rights Division of the Justice
Department, believed that it raised "very serious questions" [43]
about the validity of a wide variety of federal regulations dealing
with education, employment, and other areas of social policy. He
recommended that the Solicitor General enter the case as a friend
of the Court and throw his weight against Bakke, and behind the
University of California, in favor of affirmative action.

On the way to the Solicitor General, the recommendation
from Days made an important stop. The assistant to the SG assigned to the case was Frank Easterbrook. In the small circle of
Supreme Court–watchers, he was known both for his superb academic record at the University of Chicago Law School and for his
conservative legal views. (In 1985, when Easterbrook was thirty-
six, President Reagan appointed him to the U.S. Court of Appeals
for the Seventh Circuit, in Chicago.) Easterbrook was the first
official with a voice in the Bakke case who argued that the U.S.
government should submit a friend of the Court brief on behalf of
Bakke and against the University of California. [44]

At Davis, Easterbrook argued, there was no proof that the
medical school had previously engaged in racial discrimination
that might justify giving members of minority groups some current advantage in the admissions process to put them on an equal
footing with other candidates. And it was not enough to show that
blacks and other minorities had been discriminated against generally in society. Otherwise, he reasoned, "benign" discrimination
like the kind practiced by Davis was not benign. As far as Allan
Bakke was concerned, "he might as well have been black and
turned away on account of race." Easterbrook believed the U.S.

government could not endorse the Davis program, because it provided "gross over-compensation to minority applicants."[45]

Wade McCree was the first black elected to serve as a city judge
in Detroit. He was a judge on the United States Court of Appeals
for the Sixth Circuit before becoming Solicitor General, and he
regularly served as an envoy of the black community to establish-
ment councils. During the summer of 1977 (the first summer of the
Carter Administration and of McCree at the Justice Department),
the SG had been drawn into a dispute about another case.[46] He
didn't pay attention to Bakke until August, not long before the
brief in the Supreme Court was due. By then, the President had
given a press conference at which he said that the government's
position in the case would stand as a symbol of the new Administration's commitment to affirmative action. At the close of his
statement about the case, he added, "I might say that the Secretary
of HEW and the Attorney General, who are lawyers—and I am
not—will prepare our position."[47]

President Carter omitted the Solicitor General from the list of
lawyers preparing the government's brief, but McCree was in the
thick of it. By late summer, when lawyers in the government said
"Bakke," they referred to the fight over prestige and policy within
the Executive Branch that had developed about the case.[48] The
Justice Department was divided into two camps, one represented
by Drew Days and the Civil Rights Division and the other by
Frank Easterbrook. The memo by Easterbrook was approved by
Lawrence Wallace, the Deputy SG in charge of civil-rights cases,
and was turned into a draft brief.[49]

Just before Labor Day in 1977, the draft was leaked to *The New
York Times* and a story about it caught the attention of Joseph
Califano, the Secretary of Health, Education, and Welfare. He got
hold of the brief. In his memoirs, *Governing America*, Califano
related, "On the morning of September 6, I called Griffin Bell to
complain about the brief. He suggested that I meet with Solicitor
General Wade McCree. That meeting, the next day, was deeply
disturbing."[50] Califano went on, "McCree, who is black and had
been a judge before being appointed Solicitor General, sat with
two bright young white holdovers from the Nixon Administration. They did not disguise their distaste for affirmative
action. . . ."

The two "young white holdovers from the Nixon Administration" were Lawrence Wallace and Frank Easterbrook. (Wallace was hired in 1969 by Erwin Griswold, and Easterbrook in 1974 by Robert Bork.) At the meeting, according to Califano, one of the two younger men said he thought it was impossible to write a brief that approved a special admissions policy for the Davis medical school.

Califano: " 'Like hell it's impossible,' I said. 'I don't have any problem writing it. A lot of people in this country have worked for years to try to get equality for blacks, to develop affirmative action programs, to remedy past discrimination. We're not going to have that work thrown out the window by a couple of young lawyers.' "

Califano urged President Carter to play an active role in reshaping the Justice Department brief. In a memo to the President, marked *"Confidential"* and signed "From Joe Califano," he opened, "The draft Justice Department brief in the Bakke case is bad law, and pernicious social policy." Uncertain whether Carter would read the whole memo, Califano sent with it a handwritten note for the President's eyes only.

The second paragraph of the note read: "The brief-writing process (indeed the whole consultation process) has been so closely held—dominated through this past week by two holdover lawyers in the A.G.'s office—that even I, with a Department as deeply involved as any in the govt., with a legal background, with a presidential press statement that I would be involved, first got wind of the brief's existence in a *N.Y. Times* article over Labor Day weekend."

In the first paragraph, Califano warned: "I believe you will make the most serious mistake of your administration in domestic policy to date if you permit the Justice Department to file the *Bakke* brief in the form I read it and under present circumstances." [51]

Before Califano's memo reached the President, White House aides had already focused on the draft of the Bakke brief. Attorney General Bell told his view of the aides' involvement in his memoirs, *Taking Care of the Law.* "After a good deal of writing and rewriting McCree gave me the initial draft," he said. "I then made perhaps the biggest mistake with regard to the power centers at the

White House."[52] He took a copy of the draft when he went to see President Carter to talk about the government's position, and the President gave the copy to his counsel, Robert Lipshutz. The brief circulated to Stuart Eizenstat, the President's chief adviser on domestic policy, and other members of the staff. While the facts of the Bakke case made it a poor vehicle for a full endorsement of affirmative action by the Administration,[53] the President's aides decided anything less would amount to disapproval.

In a joint memo to the President, Eizenstat and Lipshutz contended, "The brief which the government files in the Bakke case will not simply be a legal document. Rather, it will be seen as a statement of this Administration's policy on an issue—affirmative action—which is an integral part of large numbers of Federal programs." They wanted the government to file a brief with more pronounced advocacy. "In a fundamental sense," they judged, "the brief is, in its own word, too 'dispassionate.' "[54]

On a cover page, Carter wrote:

Stu—Bob

I agree:

a) Strong affirmative action
b) no *rigid* quotas
Remanding may be ill advised—
Jump into drafting process—
J.C.

On September 12, which was the day of a Cabinet meeting, the *Times* carried a story about the Justice Department brief that reflected little of the White House deliberations. The headline read, "CARTER SAID TO BACK BAR TO RACE QUOTAS."[55] According to Califano's memoir, "That did it. I decided to raise the issue at the cabinet meeting." Andrew Young, now mayor of Atlanta, then U.S. Ambassador to the United Nations, spoke before Califano at the meeting. Young, a black who had been one of Martin Luther King, Jr.'s chief aides during the civil-rights movement, reported that the anti-quota position of the government's draft brief was seen by the civil-rights community as a "betrayal."[56] The late Patricia Roberts Harris, a black who was then

Secretary of Housing and Urban Development and a former dean of the Howard University Law School, complained that the brief was of "poor legal quality." Califano cautioned that the Bakke brief should be done "meticulously, as thousands will go over it."[57] Bell explained that Wade McCree was still working on the brief and that the President would have the chance to review it before the Justice Department submitted it to the Supreme Court. To Eizenstat, the process was now finally working as it was supposed to.[58]

Bell did not agree. He announced to the Cabinet that he doubted he would "circulate any more briefs in the future."[59] The Bakke case had taught him a lesson, and he now had a better understanding of his responsibilities as Attorney General. He had resigned from a seat on the United States Court of Appeals for the Fifth Circuit to join the Cabinet, and he believed the Justice Department should be as free from political meddling as a courthouse. The word "independent" recurred in his comments about the ideal character of the department. As in its use to describe the position of the Solicitor General, the word had a special meaning. The Attorney General recognized his duty, and the SG's, to the President. He didn't believe it was his prerogative to make government policy without regard to Administration aims. But he thought the commotion about the Bakke case had lowered the quality of the government's brief and threatened to turn it into a statement of partisan policy rather than law.[60] Bell had arrived at the view expressed later, in 1986, by Chief Justice Rehnquist: "I don't think the White House is well served by having a Solicitor General come to the Court and read the legal equivalent of a press release."[61]

How Bell acted on his commitment to the independence of the Justice Department and, in turn, to the independence of the Solicitor General during the Bakke negotiations would have surprised the President's aides if they had known about it. After a quarrelsome meeting with Eizenstat, Lipshutz, and Vice-President Walter Mondale at the White House, the Attorney General made an executive decision. As he put it in his memoirs, "Riding back to the Department of Justice, I instructed Adamson"—Terrence Adamson, one of his assistants—"not to tell McCree of the meeting or the Vice-President's comments."[62] The pressure on

McCree was "heavy enough without adding the weight of one of the White House's centers of power," and Bell decided to shelter the SG.

At the Justice Department, McCree was known for his diplomatic skills and his off-the-cuff limericks. When protectors of wildlife successfully sued the would-be builders of a dam that threatened to destroy the breeding ground of a small fish called the snail darter, the case eventually arrived in the SG's office.[63] McCree wrote:

> "Who can surpass the snail darter?
> The fish that would not be a martyr.
> It stymied the dam,
> Near the place where it swam,
> Can you think of a fish any smarter?"[64]

In 1985, McCree recalled Bakke well. "I knew Bell was taking a lot of heat on the case. The papers would speculate about it, and you know what a gossip mill Washington is. I was slow to get into the case myself, because I had another to attend to, but by the end of the summer I was in it. The Solicitor General, you may know, gives everyone with a stake in a case a chance to be heard. That is, before filing a brief, he meets with government people and others who want to be heard on the legal issues. Secretary Califano came over and made a big pitch, and we heard him out. At one point he got fairly exercised and talked about how he had dedicated his life to fighting for equal rights. When he accused Larry Wallace of undercutting the rights of blacks, Larry got all hot and said, 'Well, *some* lawyers in this room have been making a half million dollars a year representing Coca-Cola and other big corporations'—referring to what Califano pulled down before he entered government—'while the rest of us have been working in the government on behalf of civil rights.' Pat Harris, over at Housing and Urban Development, called me about this and said, 'You know, I've been black for a long time, and I know what it's like to be discriminated against.' I said, 'Pat, I've been black for longer than you have.' She said, 'I'm not just talking about biological years.' I said, 'Neither am I.' "[65]

He went on, "I talked regularly with the Attorney General

about Bakke, but I never received, directly or indirectly, a statement that the White House wanted me to do this or that. I suspect Bell did. I didn't know it at the time. But whatever directions he received he didn't transmit to me as an order. Which says to me that he wasn't *told* to tell me, because I'm certain he would have. Bell is too well disciplined a person. If the President had said, 'Tell McCree to do thus and so,' I'm sure Bell would have."

According to Bell's assistant Terrence Adamson, Bell and Adamson set up a system to handle outsiders' comments on Bakke. It worked like this: Bell told Adamson to field all suggestions about Bakke from the White House. Instead of passing them on to McCree, he was to collect them in a drawer. From time to time, Bell and Adamson would talk with McCree and others in the Justice Department about the brief. They would pass on suggestions, whether from the White House or the Attorney General, without saying who made which ones. The ideas had to succeed on their own without the advantage of sponsorship from a high office. They did not arrive on Oval Office stationery, or even on the Attorney General's, and the brief-writers were free to incorporate or reject the comments. From Bell's point of view, instead of writing what the President's aides believed they were "instructing," the Solicitor General was insulated from their direct pressure, so he could think through the law with the help of others in the Justice Department and then tell the White House what he thought the law allowed. Despite Califano's fear that McCree would be controlled by Easterbrook, the Solicitor General knew about and shared the President's belief in affirmative action.[66] But he was free to choose the argument he thought best in this case. He decided to argue that, instead of supporting Allan Bakke, the government should recommend that the Supreme Court remand the case to California so the state court could decide whether the Davis program qualified as legitimate affirmative action.[67]

When the Supreme Court handed down its decision the following June, Justice Lewis Powell began for the Court: "We speak today with a notable lack of unanimity. I will try to explain how we divided. It may not be self-evident."[68] There were six separate opinions, and enough variety in the Justices' approaches for every government faction in the Bakke fight to find cause for vindication. On the one hand, the Court ordered the University of California to admit Bakke. It found the Davis program unconstitutional, because, on the basis of race alone, the program "totally foreclosed" opportunities for people like Bakke to compete in the special admissions program. On the other hand, Justice Powell's opinion, explaining his decisive swing vote, plainly acknowledged the value of affirmative action. An opinion by Justice William Brennan pleased the government's civil-rights lawyers, because it favored affirmative-action programs on terms those lawyers had recommended. According to Califano, who also focused on Brennan's opinion, "Our arguments and persistence had made a difference. Although I was sorry to have ruffled the feelings of Bell and McCree, both of whom I liked, they could be soothed." [69]

FROM THE VANTAGE of the Solicitor General, however, the most important document to come out of the Bakke case was issued soon after the government had filed its brief with the Supreme Court and long before the Justices issued their decision. It was dated September 29, 1977, and entitled "Memorandum for the Attorney General Re: The Role of the Solicitor General." [70] Signed by the Assistant Attorney General for the Office of Legal Counsel, John Harmon, the memo was researched by Miles Foy, a former law clerk to Judge Bell. [71] It had been prompted by a controversy over the snail-darter case, memorialized by Wade McCree in his limerick, but the paper spoke directly to issues raised by Bakke. The clash between the President's legal and political advisers had moved the AG's lawyers to put their judgments on paper.

"The purpose of this memorandum," it began, "is to discuss (1) the institutional relationship between the Attorney General and the Solicitor General, and (2) the role that each should play in formulating and presenting the Government's position in litigation before the Supreme Court." [72]

The memo settled the first issue quickly. "The short of the matter," it concluded, "is that under our law the Attorney General has the power and the right to 'conduct and argue' the Government's case in any court of the United States"—and the Solicitor General worked for the AG. But the answer to the second issue

lurked in tradition as much as law, and it was harder to pin down.
The SG had enjoyed "independence" within the Justice Department and within the Executive Branch. He was not "bound" by
the views of his "clients" within the government, and he was free
to confess error, rewrite briefs, and turn down requests for petitions to the Supreme Court for four reasons: "The Solicitor General must coordinate conflicting views within the Executive
Branch; he must protect the Court by presenting meritorious
claims in a straightforward and professional manner and by screening out unmeritorious ones; he must assist in the orderly development of decisional law, and he must 'do justice'—that is, he must
discharge his office in accordance with law and ensure that improper concerns do not influence the presentation of the Government's case in the Supreme Court."

Why couldn't the Attorney General do the same? Because his
political responsibilities might "cloud a clear vision of what the law
requires." In the memo's words, "For this reason alone, in our
view, the tradition of the 'independent' Solicitor General is a wise
tradition." In the small number of cases that arose amidst political
controversy, the Attorney General could strengthen the SG's independence by taking responsibility for the final judgment on the
government's position and shielding the SG from political pressure. By preserving the Solicitor General's independence, the Attorney General enhanced the SG's ability to serve as "an officer
learned in the law."

The memo closed by addressing the most difficult question:
"How does one identify the 'rare instances' in which intervention
by the Attorney General may be justifiable?" According to the
Attorney General's aides, it was not enough that the Attorney
General disagreed with the SG over a question of law. If the SG
had made a mistake, the Supreme Court could correct him. If the
Court upheld him, "then all the better, for his legal judgment and
not that of his superiors was correct. . . . In either case," the paper
stated, "the potential benefit of intervention is usually outweighed,
in our view, by the mischief inherent in it."

About legal judgments, it was settled—the SG should be independent. "But if 'law' does not provide a clear answer to the
question presented by the case before him, we think there is no
reason to suppose that he, of all the officers in the Executive

Branch, should have the final responsibility for deciding what, as a matter of policy, the interests of the Government, the parties, or the Nation may require. To our knowledge, no Solicitor General has adopted a contrary view." So decisions about policy should be made by the Attorney General. "But the Attorney General and the President should trust the judgment of the Solicitor General not only in determining questions of law but also in distinguishing between questions of law and questions of policy. If the independent legal advice of the Solicitor General is to be preserved, it should normally be the Solicitor General who decides when to seek the advice of the Attorney General or the President in a given case."

The upshot of the Bakke case turned out to be this, the first official statement about the role of the Solicitor General in the century-old history of the office. In May of 1977, at the start of the Carter Administration, Erwin Griswold had written a letter of alarm to the Attorney General.[73] Griffin Bell had added to the hierarchy of the Justice Department an Associate Attorney General, to join the Deputy AG as one of two senior administrators. As a consequence, the Solicitor General slipped to fourth place in rank in the department—whereas he had started in 1870 in second place, with prestige almost equal to the Attorney General's. "I am concerned lest the office of the Solicitor General will be downgraded," Griswold wrote, fearing that the office would lose its authority as the government's "principal spokesman" before the Supreme Court as it gave up rank.

The memo about the role of the SG, written four months later, suggested that Griswold need not have worried about the significance of the Solicitor's loss of seniority. Commissioned by an Attorney General who was concerned about the impact on legal opinions of the process by which they were made, it was an endorsement of the SG's independence from the Attorney General and the White House by an office with a reputation for scholarship and impartiality. The Office of Legal Counsel articulated why the Solicitor General's independence was necessary if the government was to maintain and offer to the Supreme Court "a clear vision of what the law requires."

V

The Bob Jones
Case

THE FIRST PUBLIC sign of change in the Solicitor General's
office under the Reagan Administration came during February
1982, in a footnote within a brief filed by the office in the Supreme
Court. "This brief sets forth the position of the United States on
both questions presented," the note stated about a case called Bob
Jones University v. U.S. "The Acting Solicitor General fully subscribes to the position set forth on question number two, only."[1]

When the Bob Jones brief was filed, Lawrence Wallace was
Acting Solicitor General. Rex Lee, who had been sworn in as SG
seven months before, had once represented the Mormon church
when it faced a problem like Bob Jones's and, to avoid the appear-
ance of a conflict of interest, he had taken himself off the case.[2]
Wallace is otherwise the senior Deputy Solicitor and, perhaps
more self-consciously than anyone who works for the SG, he
considers it his duty to maintain the traditions of the office.[3] When
the Justices of the Supreme Court present the Court's new opinions, as they regularly do in an austere ceremony, he is often the
only lawyer for the government who attends. He sits at counsel's
table in front of the Justices, to signify that whatever the Court's
judgment, the government is prepared to comply. At the SG's
office, he minds everyone's business. This includes the minor details of submissions to the Court that he does not make. As Wallace
explains it, Justice William O. Douglas once told him how much
he appreciated that even the SG's footnotes could be relied on:
unlike the notes of some other lawyers, the SG's squarely supported the propositions for which they were cited.[4] The moral is
that Wallace feels compelled to hold the whole office to that high
standard.

The story about Justice Douglas's comment is no parable. It is common for Wallace to quote a talk with a Justice as authority for one of his maxims about the Solicitor General's office. Wallace had been editor-in-chief of the *Columbia Law Review,* an associate at Covington & Burling, a law clerk to Justice Hugo Black, and a professor at the Duke University School of Law, and, by the start of the Reagan Administration, he had been with the SG's office for thirteen years. At forty-nine, he had argued about 65 cases before the Supreme Court, [5] more than anyone else then in the government. (As of 1987, the only living advocate who had argued more cases was Erwin Griswold; his 117 put him second among twentieth-century lawyers, behind John W. Davis [140 cases], and fourth on the Supreme Court's all-time list, behind Davis, Daniel Webster [between 185 and 200], and a little-known lawyer named Walter Jones, who, between 1801 and 1850, argued 317.) [6]

Wallace knew that his footnote in the Bob Jones brief was likely to draw close attention. The disclaimer (he called it "dropping a footnote" instead of "tying a tin can") was not as extreme as Simon Sobeloff's refusal to sign the government's brief in the Peters case a generation before, but it was a strong alternative.

In some public-relations material, Bob Jones described itself as "the world's most unusual university." [7] Located in Greenville, South Carolina, the school gives "special emphasis to the Christian religion and the ethics revealed in the Holy scriptures." [8] The Reverend Billy Graham started there as a student, but transferred away because the school's ultra-fundamentalism proved too much for him. [9] In 1982, in its regular programs for those in kindergarten through graduate school, Bob Jones had approximately sixty-three hundred students. [10] In its smaller Institute of Christian Service, taught exclusively by "born again" Christians, the university had students from more than a hundred denominations, who came to learn Christian character and the principles of the Bible. [11] "The institution does not permit dancing, card playing, the use of tobacco, movie going, and other such forms of indulgences in which worldly young people often engage," a judge wrote about the university, "and no young man may walk a girl on campus unless both of them have a legitimate reason for going in the same direction." [12] During the 1980 Presidential campaign, Ronald Reagan gave a speech at Bob Jones, and called the school a "great institution." [13]

Along with another institution called Goldsboro Christian Schools, in Goldsboro, North Carolina, the university was before the Supreme Court because of its admissions policy against blacks. For most of its history, the school had excluded them. School leaders believed from their reading of Scripture that God intended the races to live separately, and they ran the university accordingly. [14] In 1970, the Internal Revenue Service ruled that Bob Jones no longer qualified for tax-exempt status because of this segregationist policy, so the school changed it. Blacks could be accepted if they were married to other blacks, or if they promised not to date or marry outside their race. After the new policy took effect, Bob Jones enrolled five blacks. By the time of the Supreme Court case, a decade later, the number of blacks attending the school was less than a dozen, making the ratio of whites to blacks about 550 to one. [15]

From the vantage point of the Solicitor General's office, the legal issue in the Bob Jones case was routine. It was a tax question. [16] After the Supreme Court called for desegregation of public schools in Brown v. Board of Education, "segregation academies" sprang up through the South. The Civil Rights Act of 1964 outlawed direct government aid to these private, whites-only schools, but the law said nothing about indirect subsidies through tax exemptions. The academies claimed to be exempt from federal tax as educational institutions under an often used section of the tax code. For a few years, the IRS excused the schools from paying Social Security, income, and other taxes, and allowed their benefactors to deduct from their own taxes the contributions they made to the schools, but by 1970, when about four hundred thousand Southern children were attending "seg academies," the agency decided to alter its stance. Doing "what we thought the law compelled us to," [17] IRS Commissioner Randolph Thrower said later, the Nixon Administration notified about five thousand schools that it would read the tax code a new way. To qualify for a tax exemption, schools had to be charitable in the broadest sense. They could not serve ends at odds with public policy. In the case of Bob

Jones University, the IRS revoked the school's exemption, on the grounds that its admissions policy contradicted the nation's commitment to halt racial discrimination.

At trial, Bob Jones won its suit against the IRS. The presiding federal district judge ruled that the university qualified for an exemption as a religious institution, despite its admissions practices. The IRS won on appeal, when the Court of Appeals rejected the lower court's "simplistic reading" of the law. [18] The university asked the Supreme Court to review the case, and Lawrence Wallace responded with another type of action peculiar to the office of Solicitor General: he "acquiesced." He agreed that the school's petition should be heard, though he opposed it on the merits. The case had drawn unusual attention from political officials in the Reagan Administration, and Wallace believed he could dampen the interest with this partial concession. [19] Like the longtime tax lawyers advising him, Wallace had no doubt the government had properly won its appeal, because the IRS ruling had been backed by the President when it was made and was amply supported by the Constitution, Supreme Court rulings, and subsequent acts of Congress. [20] But, instead of recommending that the government oppose the school's petition to the Supreme Court, which would have reduced the university's chances of being heard to about one in a hundred, he agreed that the Justices should take the case, on the grounds that many schools might be affected by the case and that the bar needed guidance from the Supreme Court.

Not long after Wallace submitted the SG's acquiescence, Congressman Trent Lott, a Republican from Mississippi, sent letters around the government protesting the Wallace position that the Court of Appeals should be upheld. His missive went to the President, the Attorney General, the Commissioner of the IRS, and Solicitor General Rex Lee. "The last time I read the Constitution," he declared, "it provided that the *Congress* is to make the laws—not appointed officials." [21] The phrase "appointed officials" covered members of the Executive Branch (including the IRS) and the Judicial Branch. Because the Court of Appeals in the Bob Jones case had upheld the IRS reading of the tax code, Lott and his supporters thought the judges were as remiss as the tax officials. One of Lott's supporters in this venture was Senator Strom Thur-

sick, helping the needy, consoling the grieved, and giving advice to the negligent. Moreover, it removes all social differences, for Muslims all stand side by side, old and young, rich and poor, high and low – equal in their submission to Allah, facing one direction, performing the same movements and recitation simultaneously.

3. Payment of Zakat

Zakat is a specified rate given willfully by well-to-do Muslims, in compliance with Allah's instructions and commandments, to their poor brothers, so as to meet their needs and save them from the humiliation caused by begging. It is incumbent on every Muslim who owns the minimum amount of wealth liable to payment of zakat. The Qur'aan states, (the meaning of which is translated as):

> "And they were commanded not, but that they should worship Allah, keeping religion pure for Him, as men by nature upright, and to establish prayer and to pay the poor-due (zakat). That is true religion." (The Qur'aan, Chapter Al-Baiyina, 98:5)

Those who deny zakat will commit an act of disbelief because they deprive the rightful recipients of zakat, including the poor and the needy, of their rights. Therefore, the first Caliph, Abu Bakr, may Allah be pleased with him, fought those who refused to pay zakat after the Prophet's death, and uttered his well-known statement:

> "By Allah! If they hold back from me even equal to a rein for a camel which they paid during the days of the Prophet, peace be upon him, then I shall fight against them for holding back this reign."

Zakat is not, as claimed by some people who are unfamiliar with Islam, a tax levied by the Islamic State on its subjects. If it had been a tax it would have been collected by all of the population of the Islamic State, both Muslims and non-Muslims. In the case of zakat, however, it is required only of Muslims, it is not considered an obligation for non-Muslims.

The conditions and prerequisites of zakat as prescribed by Islam are as follows:

1. To have the minimum amount of money or property liable to payment of zakat (i.e. nisab) provided it is in

excess of one's basic needs, namely: food, clothing, drink and residence.

2. Expiry of one year after the beginning of ownership; otherwise no zakat shall be paid.

Recipients of zakat are defined in the Noble Qur'aan, (the meaning of which is translated as):

"The alms (i.e.: zakat) are only for the poor and the needy, and those who collect them, and those whose hearts are to be reconciled (newly converted Muslims), and to free the captives and the debtors, and for the cause of Allah, and (for) the wayfarers; a duty imposed by Allah. Allah is All-Knower, All-Wise."(The Qur'aan, Chapter At-Tauba, 9:60)

It is estimated at a percentage of 2.5%. By imposing it, Islam aims at uprooting poverty from society and dealing with its resulting dangers, such as robbery, murder, indecent assaults (like rape), as well as reviving the spirit of cooperation and social solidarity among Muslims by satisfying the needs of the poor and the destitute and helping debtors. If we read the Prophet's Hadith (pbuh):

"A neighborhood in which one suffers from hunger will be deprived of Allah's protection." (Imam Ahmad)

Then the concept of zakat becomes clear. The difference between zakat and tax is seen in the fact that zakat is generally paid by a Muslim willingly without the need to compel him to do that. Moreover, its very name suggests purifying the souls of the rich of miserliness and avarice that induce them to forget their needy and poor brothers. The Qur'aan says,(the meaning of which is translated as):

"And whoever is saved from his own greed, such are the successful." (The Qur'aan, Chapter At-Tagabun, 64:16)

Zakat also purifies the hearts of poor people of hate and envy for the rich, especially when they see them pay the prescribed percentage and attend to them with kindness and generosity.

Allah has warned those who refuse to pay zakat, by saying, (the meaning of which is translated as):

"And let not those who hoard up that which Allah has bestowed upon them of His bounty think that it is better for them. Nay, it is worse for them. That which they hoard will be their collar on the Day of Resurrection..." (The Qur'aan, Chapter Ali 'Imran, 3:180)

The Prophet, (pbuh) said in this regard:

"A wealthy person who has gold and silver, but does not pay the zakat due on them, (should know that) his gold and silver will be melted on the Day of Judgement and converted into slabs which will then be heated in the fire of Hell, and then his forehead, his sides, and his back will be branded therewith. Whenever these slabs get cold, they will be heated up once more (in the furnace of the Hell), the branding will be continued throughout the day, the duration of which will be equal to fifty thousand years, and the cases of all the people will have been decided by this time and they will be shown their way either to the Hell or to Paradise." (Muslim)

4. Fasting During Ramadan

It is one month of the lunar calendar during which Muslims abstain from food, drinks, and sexual intercourse in the daytime, i.e. from dawn up to sunset, in accordance with the Qur'aanic verse, (the meaning of which is translated as):

"O you who believe! Fasting is prescribed for you as it was prescribed for those before you, that you may ward off (evil)." (The Qur'aan, Chapter Al-Baqarah, 2:183).

Fasting is not limited to abstinence from tangible things that break it. It has a wider scope that includes, as well, such moral evils as telling lies, backbiting, tale-bearing, cheating, deceit, nonsense etc. It is to be borne in mind that such bad habits must be avoided at all times. However, this requirement is emphasized in the month of Ramadan, as pointed out in the Hadith of the Prophet (pbuh):

"If a person does not refrain from lying and indecent activities, Allah does not want that he should abstain from eating and drinking." (Bukhari, Abu Dawud & Tirmidhi)

Fasting is a form of strife between the human soul and its desires and whims. It has social benefits explained in the following Hadith of the Prophet (pbuh):

"When anyone of you is fasting, he should abstain from loose talk and the noisy exchange of words. If someone starts cursing him or picks up a quarrel with him, he should tell him that 'I am fasting.' (Bukhari & Muslim)

Fasting also makes a Muslim feel the needs of his poor brothers who do not get sufficient food, clothing or housing and therefore he inquires about their conditions, seeing to their needs and requirements.

5. Hajj (Pilgrimage)

Hajj is a journey to the Sacred Mosque in Makkah for the performance of specific acts at specified times. This fifth pillar of Islam is obligatory, once in a lifetime for every Muslim who has reached the age of puberty, male or female, provided they are physically, financially and mentally capable. A sick Muslim with a terminal disease preventing the performance of Hajj, having the financial ability, should hire someone to perform Hajj on his or her behalf. Also a poor person who does not have sufficient money for the Hajj trip, in excess of his basis needs and the needs of his family, is exempt from Hajj. The Qur'aan states, (the meaning of which is translated as):

"...And Pilgrimage to the House (of Allah) is a duty unto Allah for mankind, for him who can bear the journey. As for him who disbelieves (let him know that) Lo! Allah is Independent of (all) creatures." (The Qur'aan, Chapter Ali 'Imran, 3:97)

Hajj is the largest Islamic congregation in which Muslims from everywhere gather at one place, at one time, to pray unto One Lord. They put on uniform dress, perform the same rites, repeating one utterance:

"Here I am at your Service, O Allah, here I am at your service. Here I am. There is no partner with you. Here I am. Verily, all praise and grace is Yours, and the sovereignty too. There is no partner with you."

It is as if the pilgrims are saying, 'O Allah! We have come to this place in compliance with your call, seeking your pleasure and acknowledging your Oneness, and that you alone are worthy of sincere worship."

In Hajj, there is no difference or discrimination between the rich and the poor, the high and the low, the black and the white, the Arab and the non-Arabs --- all are equal in the before Allah. Only righteousness differentiates between people. This helps to confirm brotherly relations between Muslims and unify their feelings and hopes.

Another benefit of such devotional activity is that related to belief. Belief in the necessity of this form of worship is obligatory, since it was contained in the scriptures revealed by Allah, and Prophets were commanded to convey it and call people to believe in it without compulsion. Conviction is a must, for coercion makes a man proclaim with his tongue what is in conflict with what he hides in his mind or heart, and that is, in fact, hypocrisy condemned by Islam and deemed to be worse than disbelief. In several verses, the Qur'aan made it clear that Prophet's mission is limited to guidance of people to good and conveyance of the divine message. It states, (the meaning of which is translated as):

"... but if you turn away, then the duty of Our Messenger is only to convey (the message) plainly." (The Qur'aan, Chapter At-Tagabun, 64:12)

Yet calling to the way of Allah, glory be to Him, should be in the best manner as stated in the Qur'aan, (the meaning of which is translated as):

"Call unto the way of your Lord with wisdom and fair exhortation, and argue with them in the better way..." (The Qur'aan, Chapter An-Nahl, 16:125)

Guidance is from Allah only, as stated in the Qur'aan, (the meaning of which is translated as):

"Lo! You (O Muhammad) guide not whom you love, but Allah guides whom He wills." (The Qur'aan, Chapter Al-Qasas, 28:56)

Such devotions are defined as the 'Fundamentals of Faith' and the faith, or belief, of a Muslim can never be complete unless he believes in all of them. Therefore whoever denies any of them is a disbeliever in all of the religion.

Fundamentals of Faith

1. Belief in Allah

It is the belief in the existence of Allah and in the truth that He, alone is the Creator, the Provider, the Giver of Life and Cause of Death. That He is the Creator and Arranger of all things in the Universe; only what He wills can exist; He has no partner in His Lordship or Divinity. The Qur'aan says, (the meaning of which is translated as):

> *"...His verily is all creation and commandment. Blessed be Allah, The Lord of the Worlds!" (The Qur'aan, Chapter Al-A'raf, 7:54)*

He is the Only God Worthy of Worship; in Him alone trust is to be put, and to Him only invocations, vows and devotions are to be directed. He, glory be to Him, has the most beautiful and perfect attributes stated in the Qur'aan or the Prophet's traditions. None of His creatures is like Him in relation to His attributes. No physical interpretation or invalidation of the divine attributes is to be entertained. Nothing is similar, comparable, or equivalent to Him. He is free from all imperfections. That is made clear in the Noble Qur'aan, (the meaning of which is translated as):

> *"... There is nothing whatsoever like unto Him, and He is the All-Hearer, All-Knower." (The Qur'aan, Chapter Ash-Shura, 42:11)*

2. Belief in Angels

It is the belief that Allah, glory to Him, has created creatures known as angels whose total number is known only to Allah. He has created them to serve and worship Him. He says, (the meaning of which is translated as):

> *"The Messiah will never scorn to be a servant of Allah, nor will the favored angels..." (The Qur'aan, Chapter An-Nisa'a, 4:172)*

He has also created them to perform the tasks assigned to them by Allah, He said, (the meaning of which is translated as):

"...A Fire... over which are set angels strong (stern), severe, who resist not Allah in that which He commands them, but do that which they are commanded." (The Qur'aan Chapter At-Tahrim, 66:6)

Those angels are not rivals to Allah, nor are they His children, Allah said, (the meaning of which is translated as):

"And they Say: 'The Most Beneficent has taken unto Himself a son. Glorious is He! Nay, but (those whom they call sons) are honored servants; They speak not until He has spoken, and they act by His command." (The Qur'aan, Chapter Al-Anbiya', 26:27)

Allah, Glory to Him, has told us about the names and tasks of some of the angels, but He has not told us about others. Nevertheless, we are required to believe in them all. Among the angels, there are:

- Gabriel, peace be upon him, who is assigned the task of conveying Allah's revelations to His prophets.

- Michael, peace be upon him, who is in charged of the affairs of rain.

- The Angel of Death, peace be upon him, who is designated to take man's soul at death.

- Israfil, peace be upon him, who is in charged of blowing the trumpet at the end of this world when everybody's soul is taken away, and again at the time of resurrection.

- Ridwan, peace be upon him, keeper of the Garden (Paradise).

- Malik, peace be upon him, keeper of the Hell-fire.

- The Guards of Hell (Zabaniyah), responsible for punishing and tormenting the dwellers of Hell.

- The two angels for each person, one of which is charged with writing down all good deeds, and the other with writing down all evil deeds.

There are other angels who do whatever they are instructed by Allah to do. They are obedient to Allah – they never disobey Allah's commands, but do that which they are commanded. According to the Prophet's (pbuh) description. He (pbuh) said:

"Angels were created from light, Jinns from burning fire, and Adam was created from that thing which you have already been told." (Muslim)

Although they were created from invisible light, they have been given the ability to take different shapes in which they can be seen. In the Noble Qur'aan we read about Mary, (the meaning of which is translated as):

"And she chose seclusion from them. Then We sent unto her Our spirit (Gabriel), and he assumed for her the likeness of a perfect man. She said: 'Lo! I seek refuge in the All-Beneficent One from you, if you are God-fearing.' He said: 'I am only a messenger of your Lord, that I may bestow on you a faultless son.'" (The Qur'aan, Chapter Maryam, 19:17-19)

Angels have wings. Some angels have two wings, some have three, others have more. The Qur'aan describes them by the following verse, (the meaning of which is translated as):

"Praise be to Allah, the Creator of the Heavens and the earth, Who made the angels messengers with wings – two, three and four. He increases in creation what He wills..." (The Qur'aan Chapter Fatir, 35:1)

There are many other details about them that are only known to Allah.

3. Belief in Divine Books
It is the belief that Allah revealed sacred scriptures to His messengers to covey them to people. Of those books or scriptures are the following:

- The Scriptures of Ibrahim (Abraham) and Moses, peace be upon them, some of whose teachings are indicated in the Noble Qur'aan, (the meaning of which is translated as):

"Or has he not been informed of what is in the scriptures of Moses, and of Ibrahim (Abraham), who fulfilled (what he was commanded), That no laden one shall bear another's load, and that man has only that for which he makes effort,

and that his effort will be seen. And afterward he will be repaid for it with the fullest payment." (The Qur'aan, Chapter An-Najm, 53:36-41)

- The Torah, which is the holy book revealed to Moses, Allah said, (the meaning of which is translated as):

"Lo! We did revealed the Torah, wherein is guidance and a light, by which the Prophets, who submitted themselves to Allah's Will, judged for the Jews, and the rabbis and the priests (judged) by such of Allah's Scripture as they were bidden to observe and thereunto were they witnesses. So fear not mankind, but fear Me. And barter not My revelations for a little gain. Whoever judges not by that which Allah has revealed: such are disbelievers." (The Qur'aan Chapter Al-Ma'idah, 5:44)

The Noble Qur'aan has conveyed some of the content of the Torah, including some aspects of Prophet Muhammad's character. It states, (the meaning of which is translated as):

"Muhammad is the Messenger of Allah and those with him are hard on the disbelievers and merciful among themselves. You see them bowing and falling prostrate, seeking bounty from Allah and (His) acceptance. The mark of them is on their foreheads from the trace of prostration. Such is their likeness in the Torah..." (The Qur'aan, Chapter Al-Fath, 48:29)

The Noble Qur'aan has also indicated some of the jurisprudence rulings contained in the Torah, (the meaning of which is translated as):

"And We prescribed for them therein: A life for a life, and an eye for an eye, and a nose for a nose, and a ear for a ear, and a tooth for a tooth, and for wounds, retaliation. But whoever forgoes it (in the way of charity) it shall be expiation for him. Whoever judges not by that which Allah has revealed such are wrong-doers." (The Qur'aan, Chapter Al-Ma'idah, 5:45)

- The Psalms, revealed to David. The Qur'aan says, (the meaning of which is translated as):

"... and as We imparted unto David the Psalms." (The Qur'aan, Chapter An-Nisa'a, 4:163)

- The Gospel, revealed to Jesus ('Issa). The Qur'aan says, (the meaning of which is translated as):

"And We caused Jesus, son of Mary, to follow in their footsteps, confirming that which was (revealed) before him, and We bestowed on him the Gospel, wherein is guidance and a light confirming that which was (revealed) before it in the Torah – a guidance and an admonition unto those who fear Allah." (The Qur'aan, Chapter Al-Ma'idah, 5:46)

The existing Gospels, in the hands of people, are in fact, not the word of Allah or Jesus, but the words of his followers and disciples, in which they incorporated a many of his biographical stories, exhortations and commandments, and introduced many distortions, changes and falsifications in order to serve certain purposes.

According to the T. Tacker,[9] the Gospels were introduced to reflect a clear concept of the practical requirements of the community for whom they were written. Frequently material has been employed in them without the slightest concern about transforming them or distorting them.

A Muslim is required to believe in the Gospel as the Word of Allah, but not this one in the hands of people nowadays; it is the authentic Gospel revealed to Jesus, peace be upon him, that the Muslim must believe in. He is not required to follow it or put it to action because it was revealed for a certain group of people at a specific period of time. Jesus said:

"I am not sent but unto the lost sheep of the house of Israel." (Matthew 15:24)

The Noble Qur'aan indicated some hints in the Gospel that foretold of Muhammad's prophethood, (the meaning of which is translated as):

"And My Mercy encompasses all things, therefore I shall ordain it for those who ward off (evil) and pay the poor-due, and those who believe in Our revelations; Those who follow the Messenger, the Prophet who can neither read nor write, whom they will find described in the Torah and the Gospel

---

[9] See "Islam and Messianism" by 'Aziz Samad.

(which are) with them. He will enjoin on them that which is right and forbid them that which is wrong. He will make lawful for them (all) good things and prohibit for them (only) the evils; and he will relieve them of their burden and the fetters that they used to wear..." (The Qur'aan, Chapter Al-A'raf, 156:157)

The Noble Qur'aan also pointed out that both the Gospel and the Torah, before it, had exhorted jihad (i.e.:fighting) in the way of Allah in order to exalt His Word, He said, (the meaning of which is translated as):

"Lo! Allah has bought from the believers their lives and their wealth so that the Garden will be theirs. They fight in the way of Allah and slay and are slain. It is a promise which is binding on Him in the Torah and the Gospel and the Qur'aan. Who fulfils his covenant better than Allah? Rejoice then in your bargain that you have made, for that is the supreme triumph." (The Qur'aan, Chapter At-Tauba, 9:111)

• The Glorious Qur'aan: It must be believed that it is the Word of Allah revealed through Gabriel, peace be upon him, unto Muhammad, blessing and peace be upon him, and that it is the last of the Revealed Scriptures. It differs from preceding scriptures in the following ways:

• It is the last of the Revealed Books. Therefore, Allah – Glory to Him, has promised to preserve it for humanity till the end of this world, and no addition or deletion has occurred to it, as He has declared, (the meaning of which is translated as):

"Lo! We, even We, have revealed the Reminder (i.e.:the Qur'aan), and Lo! We verily are its Guardian." (The Qur'aan, Chapter Al-Hijr, 15:9)

• Its recitation is one aspect of worship.

• It embraces all laws and regulations on which a virtuous society can be founded. According to J. S. Restler (a contemporary French Scholar and Professor at the Islamic Institute, Paris), in his book, "The Arab Civilization":

"The Qur'aan finds answers to all issues and establishes the link between the religious and the moral law. It aims to create order and social consolidation and to alleviate distress, hard-heartedness and remove superstition. It seeks to help the oppressed and enjoins mercy and kindness. With respect to legislation, it has laid rules and directives for daily cooperation and organized contracting and inheritance. As for family, it has identified for everyone forms of conduct towards children, captives, animals, health, clothing, etc."

• It is a historical document that shows the sequence of events and respective revelations for all messengers of Allah since Adam up to Muhammad, peace be upon them all.

• It was revealed for all mankind, not only for the Arabs, as indicated in the following verse, (the meaning of which is translated as):

"Alif, Lam, Ra, (This is) a scripture which We have revealed unto you (Muhammad) that thereby you may bring forth mankind from darkness unto light, by the permission of their Lord..." (The Qur'aan, Chapter Ibrahim, 14:1)

4. Belief in the Messengers of Allah

It is the belief that Allah, Glory to Him, has chosen from mankind prophets and messengers. He revealed scriptures to the messengers to convey them to people so that they should have no plea against Allah. As for prophets, they did not receive scriptures or convey a new religious law; but they were sent by Allah only to confirm and preach the law of prophets and messengers who preceded them. There were many Prophets and messengers; only Allah knows their real number. The Qur'aan states, (the meaning of which is translated as):

"Verily We sent messengers before thee, among them those of whom We have told you, and some of whom We have not told you..." (The Qur'aan, Chapter Al-Mu'min, 40:78)

Those prophets and messengers were all human beings, as stated in the Qur'aan, (the meaning of which is translated as):

"Say: 'I am only a man like you, to whom has been revealed that your God is only One God. And Whoever hopes for the

*meeting with his Lord, let him do righteous work and make
none to share int the worship due of his Lord.'" (The
Qur'aan, Chapter Al-Kahf, 18:110).*

The Glorious Qur'aan tells us about Jesus, peace be upon him, (the
meaning of which is translated as):

*"The Messiah, son of Mary, was no more than a messenger.
Messengers (the like of whom) had passed away before him.
And his mother was a supporter of truth. And they both used
to eat (earthly) food. See how We make the signs clear for
them, and yet see how they are turned away!" (The Qur'aan,
Chapter Al-Ma'idah, 5:75)*

The Qur'aan has mentioned the names of twenty-five prophets and
messengers:

*"That is Our argument, We gave it unto Abraham against
his folk. We raise unto degrees (of wisdom) whom We will.
Lo! Your Lord is All-Wise, Well-Aware. And We bestowed
upon him, Isaac and Jacob, each of them We guided; and
Noah did We guide aforetime; and of his seed (We guided)
David and Solomon and Job and Joseph and Moses and
Aaron. Thus do We reward the good. And Zachariah and
John and Jesus and Elias. Each one (of them) was of the
righteous. And Ishmael and Elisha and Jonah and Lot. Each
on of them did We prefer above (Our) creatures (of their
times)." (The Qur'aan, Chapter Al-An'am, 6:83-86)*

About Adam, peace be upon him, the Qur'aan says, (the meaning of
which is translated as):

*Lo! Allah, preferred Adam and Noah and the Family of
Abraham and the Family of 'Imran above the peoples (of
their times)." (The Qur'aan, Chapter Ali 'Imran, 3:33)*

About Hud, peace be upon him, the Qur'aan says, (the meaning of
which is translated as):

*"And unto (the tribe of) 'Aad (We sent) their brother, Hud.
He said: 'O my people! worship Allah! You have no other
God save Him...'" (The Qur'aan, Chapter Hud, 11:50)*

About Shu'ayb, peace be upon him, the Qur'aan says, (the meaning
of which is translated as):

"And unto Midian (We sent) their brother Shu'ayb. He said:O my people! worship Allah. You have no other God save Him..." (The Qur'aan, Chapter Hud, 11:84)

About Idris, peace be upon him, the Qur'aan says, (the meaning of which is translated as):

"And (mention) Ishmail, and Idris, and Dhul-Kifl. All were of the steadfast." (The Qur'aan, Chapter Al-Anbiya', 21:85)

And about Muhammad, (pbuh):

"Muhammad is the Messenger of Allah. And those with him are hard against the disbelievers and merciful among themselves..." (The Qur'aan, Chapter Al-Fatah, 48:29)

The belief in all prophets is imperative, if one believes in some of them and rejects others he will be deemed a disbeliever. This is pointed out in the Qur'aan, (the meaning of which is translated as):

"Lo! Those who disbelieve in Allah and His messengers, and seek to make distinction between Allah and His messengers, and Say: "We believe in some and disbelieve in others," and seek to choose a way in between; such are disbelievers in truth; and for disbelievers We have prepared a shameful doom." (The Qur'aan, Chapter An-Nisa'a, 4:150-151)

The first of those messengers was Adam and the last was Muhammad; therefore, there is no prophet or messenger after him.

5. Belief in the Hereafter

It is firm belief in the fact that this world will come to an end and perish one day. The Qur'aan states, (the meaning of which is translated as):

"Every one that is thereon will pass away. There remains but the Face of your Lord full of Might and Glory." (The Qur'aan, Chapter Ar-Rahman, 55:26-27)

This also includes the belief that a day will follow on which Allah resurrects all creatures from their tombs to be paid their due. Those who did good will be rewarded for their good, while those who did evil will be punished for their evil deeds. The Qur'aan gives several instances in which Allah explains the possibility of resurrection:

Contemplating the revival of dead earth by the crops He produces therefrom, Allah said, (the meaning of which is translated as):

"...And you see the earth barren, but when We send down water thereon, it stimulates and swells and brings forth every lovely kind (of growth). That is because Allah, He is the Truth and because He is Able to do all things; and because the Hour will come, there is no doubt thereof; and because Allah will raise those who are in the grave..." (The Qur'aan, Chapter Al-Hajj, 22:5-7)

Contemplating the creation of the heavens and the earth, which is greater than the creation of man, Allah said, (the meaning of which is translated as):

"Have they not seen that Allah, Who created the heavens and the earth and was not wearied by their creation, is able to give life to the dead? Aye, He verily is ever Able to do all this." (The Qur'aan, Chapter Al-Ahqaf, 46:33)

Reflecting on how man sleeps and awakens, as if it is life after death. In this vein, sleep is call the 'minor death.' Allah said, (the meaning of which is translated as):

"Allah takes souls at the time of their death, and those which die not (He takes) during their sleep. He keeps those (souls) for which He has ordained death and dismisses the rest till an appointed term. Lo! Herein verily are portents for people who take thought." (The Qur'aan, Chapter Az-Zumar, 39:42)

Considering the first creation of man, Allah said, (the meaning of which is translated as):

"And he (man) has coined for Us a similitude, and forgotten the fact of his creation, saying: 'Who will revive these bones when they have rotten away?' Say: 'He will revive them Who produced them at the first, for He is All-Knower of every creature.'" (The Qur'aan, Chapter Ya-Sin, 36:78-79)

Believing in the Hereafter involves belief in the interval between the worldly life and the Hereafter, during which those who do good enjoy bliss and comfort, while the those who do evil suffer punishment. It also involves belief in resurrection after death, as well as assembly, judgement, testimony of man's limbs, reckoning, the the Bridge across Hell, recompense by Paradise or Hell-Fire, and eternal, never-ending life in the Hereafter. The Qur'aan states, (the meaning of which is translated as):

> "Lo! Those who disbelieve, among the people of the Scripture and the idolaters, will abide in fire of hell. They are the worst of created beings. (And) Lo! Those who believe and do good works are the best of created beings. Their reward is with their Lord: Gardens of Eden beneath which rivers flow, wherein they dwell forever. Allah is pleased with and they are pleased with Him. This is for him who fears his Lord." (The Qur'aan, Chapter Al-Baiyina, 98:6-8)

6. Belief in the Divine Decree and the Divine Will

It is the firm belief that Allah always knew all things before they took place and how they would be. Then He brought things into existence in accordance with His unlimited knowledge and apportioning. This is stated in the Noble Qur'aan, (the meaning of which is translated as):

> "...He has created everything and has meted out for it a measure." (The Qur'aan, Chapter Al-Furqan, 25:2)

Whatever happened or happens throughout existence is known to Allah before it happens, then it takes place in accordance with the Will and Decree. The Prophet (pbuh) said:

> "No one shall be deemed a believer unless he believes in divine destiny, whether for the good or harm (of man), and he must believe that what happened to him would never have missed him, and what missed him would never have happened to him." (Tirmidhi)

This should not preclude using the right or required means to achieve his aims. For example, a man who wishes to have children should act and resort to marriage, which is the means or method that would realize this for him. However this may or may not bring about the desired results, as Allah wills, because it is not the causes that bring about effects by themselves; it is the Will of Allah that makes means or causes work. In fact causes are created and ordained by Allah, Glory to Him.

In this context, the Prophet, peace be upon him, was asked about invocations and medications whether they can ward off anything preordained by Allah. He said: *"They are part of Allah's preordainment."*

Hunger, thirst and cold are aspects of Allah's preordainment, and people try to ward off hunger by eating food, thirst by drinking water, and cold by warming themselves. So they defend themselves against what is preordained for them (hunger, thirst and cold) by what is preordained for them (food, drink and warmth). This means that they ward off the preordainment with the preordainment.

Belief in Divine Destiny, after use of means and causes, has many advantages, including:

Acceptance and contentment with preordained events or things results in peace of mind, which rids the heart or mind of concerns and sorrow for what happens or what is lost. It is well-known that lack of content and satisfaction may lead to many diseases and disorders, whereas belief in Divine Destiny relieves the human souls of the effects of unrest and anxiety. The Glorious Qur'aan makes this clear in this verse, (the meaning of which is translated as):

"No calamity befalls on the earth or in yourselves but it is inscribed in the Book of Decrees before We bring it into existence. Verily, that is easy for Allah. In order that you may not grieve at the things that you fail to get, nor rejoice over that which has been given to you. Allah likes not prideful boasters." (The Qur'aan, Chapter Al-Hadid, 57:22-23)

An invitation to seek knowledge and explore the secrets and reserves or resources of the Universe. What is preordained for man, such as illness, moves him to look for medication or cure that helps him to save himself by preordained cure from predestined illness.

Alleviate man's calamities. If a person undergoes loss of money or trade, such loss is a disaster for him, but if he gives in to grief, the disaster will be doubled for him. But if he believes truly in Divine Destiny he will be relieved and content, as he is aware that it is inescapable. The Noble Prophet (pbuh) guides us in this respect by saying:

"Stick to what is useful to you, work, do well, seek help from Allah and never give in. If anything befalls you, just say: 'Allah has preordained and done what He has willed.' Do not say: 'If only..' because it opens the way for the devil's work."

Belief in Divine Destiny is not, as some would think, an invitation to helpless dependence and lack of activity. The Noble Prophet (pbuh) urges us to the contrary by saying:

"If one of you takes his rope to gather a bundle of wood and then sells it, it would be better for him than to beg from people, whether they give, or refuse to give him."

He (pbuh), said to the person who asked him about his riding animal which he had left without tying or hobbling it under the pretext of trust in Allah:

"Restrain it and trust (Allah)."

The Political Aspect of Islam

The Islamic legislation in the political domain, as in other domains, has introduced basic principles and general rules that constitute the nucleus of the Muslim State. The ruler of the Muslim State is considered an agent that implements the commands of Allah through the implementation of these rules and principles. The Noble Qur'aan says, (the meaning of which is translated as):

"Whoever judges not by that which Allah has revealed; such are the disbelievers" (The Qur'aan, Chapter Al-Ma'idah, 5:44)

The ruler of the Muslim State is representative of the whole nation delegated to perform the following:

1. To do his best to provide honest and honorable ways of living for them, as stated by the Prophet Muhammad (pbuh), (the meaning of which is translated as):

"If a person is made to look after some affairs of the Muslims, but fails to work for their cause and their welfare as he does for himself, he will not get even the aroma of the Paradise." (Al-Tabarani)

The ruler of the Muslim State must be as described by the Caliph 'Umar Ibn Al-Khattab, may Allah be pleased with him, when he said to his companions; "Guide me to a man whom I can assign to take care of certain affairs of the Muslims which are of concern to me." They mentioned Abdur-Rahman Ibn 'Auf. He said, "He is weak." They mentioned another one and he did not approve of him. Then they asked, "Who do you want?" He said: "I want a man who, when appointed a governor, he behaves as if he was one of them, and even when he is not their leader, he appears as if he were their leader." They said; "We think Ar-Rabi'a Ibn Al-Harith is the one." 'Umar said, "You are right", and he appointed him.

2. Not to appoint in authority over the Muslims anyone who is not up to bearing responsibility or trust, such as when he favors a friend or a relative more than worthier people to the position. Abu Bakr, the first Caliph, said to Yazeed Ibn Sufyan when he sent him to Syria, *"O Yazeed! You have relatives and you may favor them more than others*

with the rank of governor, which makes me most worried about you."
Allah's Messenger (pbuh) said:

> *"If one is placed in authority over the Muslims and he appoints some one over them, favoring him due to his relationship with him, Allah's curse be upon him and no acts shall be accepted from him until Allah throws him into Hell." (Bukhari & Muslim).*

The aforesaid rules and principles are characterized by the following;

- They are divine, ordained by Allah. According to them, all are equal; the ruler and the ruled, the rich and the poor, the noble and the lowly, the black and the white – no one, however high-ranking, is to violate them or pass laws that are in conflict with them. 'Umar Ibn Al-Khattab, may Allah be pleased with them, said in this regard: *"The Commander of the Faithful (i.e.:the Caliph) is one of you, but he is the most heavy-laden among you."*

All are required to respect these rules and principles and to demand their implementation by both the ruler and the ruled. In Islam there is no absolute power for any human, even the rulers' powers are governed by the Law. In case he has a compliant with the Law, he has no right to being heard or obeyed. The Prophet (pbuh) said, (the meaning of which is translated as):

> *"It is obligatory upon a Muslim to listen and obey (the authority) whether he likes it or not; save when he is asked to do something sinful. If he is asked to do a sinful act, then there is no hearing or obedience." (Bukhari & Muslim).*

Consultation is the pivot of the political system of Islam. The Qur'aan refers to this basic element by saying, (the meaning of which is translated as):

> *"It was by the mercy of Allah that you were lenient with them (O Muhammad), for if you had been stern and fierce of heart they would have dispersed from round about you. So pardon them and ask forgiveness for them and consult with them upon the conduct of affairs." (The Qur'aan, Ali 'Imran, 3:159)*

In the former verse, consultation is mentioned side by side with prayer, the pillar of Islam, thereby gaining prominence. The counsel of wise knowledgeable people should be sought in everything that relates to the nation's interests. At the end of the verse, Allah, glory to Him, praises the believers in general in view of their commitment to consultation in all their affairs.

In the latter verse, Allah, the Exalted, instructs His Messenger, who was the Sovereign of the Muslim State, to seek counsel in those matters related to the interests and affairs of the people if no judgment or verdict was revealed by Allah about them. However if there is a clear text containing a verdict, it will not be subject to consultation. Allah's Messenger used to consult his companions as stated by Abu Hurairah, may Allah be pleased with him; *"I have never seen a person who is more keen on consulting his companions than Allah's Messenger, peace be upon him."* (Al-Tirmidhi)

Several events indicated that the Prophet, peace be upon him, changed his mind after he had consulted his companions.

Jurisprudence considered it obligatory for the ruler to consult the people about matters relating their interests. Even if he neglects consultation, people are required to insist on their right to say their word and give their opinion. That is based on the above mentioned verses, because the Islamic Law considers the ruler a representative (of the nation) who is responsible to perform what is delegated to him. The people, in return, are required to control the ruler's implementation of the Law. Islam gives everyone the freedom of opinion and criticism in the manner he deems appropriate. The Gracious Prophet, (pbuh) said:

"Whoever among you notices something evil should correct it with his own hands, and if he is unable to do so, he should prohibit the same with his tongue, and if he is unable even to do this, he should at least consider it as bad in his heart; this is the lowest degree of faith." (Muslim).

It even considers opinion-giving a duty, as indicated in the following Hadith, (the meaning of which is translated as):

"The best Jihad (struggle in the cause of Allah) is to utter a word of justice before a tyrannical ruler." (Abu Dawood & Tirmidhi).

This opinion-giving, however, should be within the limits of constructive criticism, away from slander, insult and trouble making. Abu Bakr addressed people, saying:

> *"O people! I have been appointed as your ruler though I am not the best among you. So If you find me in the right, just help me. But if you find me in the wrong, just correct me. Obey me so long as I obey Allah in conducting your affairs. However, if I disobey Him I have no claim to your obedience."*

'Umar Ibn Al-Khattab, one day stood on the pulpit addressing people: *"O people! If you find that I have some crookedness, correct me."* One bedouin rose to his feet and said: *"By Allah! If we find you crooked, we will correct you with our swords."* Yet 'Umar did not get angry or harbor malice towards him, he only raised his hands towards the heaven and said:

> *"Praise be to Allah, Who has created among our people a person who is able to correct the crookedness of 'Umar."*

The ruler was even called to account. Once, 'Umar addressed people while having a two-piece dress on. When he said:

> *"O people! Listen and obey."* A man stood up and said: *"No listening! No obedience!"* 'Umar asked why. The man answered: *"Because you have a two-piece dress while we have only a single one."* 'Umar at once called out: *"Abdullah Ibn 'Umar! Tell them."* Abdullah said: *"I gave him my garment."* The man then said: *"Now listen and obey."*

Thus Islam preserved rights and protected public and private freedoms. It kept the sources of legislation away from the narrow-scooped whims and desires of legislators, as their legislation is the outcome of personal or regional needs and circumstances. What was legislated yesterday is invalidated today, and what is legislated today is likely to be invalidated tomorrow. Islam has not legislated for other partial issues and affairs. It aims to leave the door open for Muslims to lay down proper rules and regulations that suit their conditions and meet their requirements and interests anywhere and at any time, provided such rules and regulations are not in conflict with the principles and fundamentals of Islam.

The Military Aspect of Islam

In principle, Islam considers peace and reconciliation the basis of relations with other nations, considering that the word "Islam" means "peace". Islam, however, prescribes and considers war lawful, after exhausting all means of promoting peace, only in three cases, namely;

1. Self-defense, i.e., defense of one's body, family and country. The Qur'aan says, (the meaning of which is translated as):

   "And fight in the Way of Allah those who fight you, but transgress not the limits. Truly, Allah likes not the transgressors." (The Qur'aan, Al-Baqarah, 2:190)

2. To save people from injustice and oppression, Allah said, (the meaning of which is translated as):

   "And what is wrong with you that you fight not in the cause of Allah, and for those weak, ill-treated and oppressed among men, women and children, whose cry is: 'Our Lord! Rescue us from this town whose people are oppressors, and raise for us from You one who will protect, and raise for us from You one who will help.'" (The Qur'aan, An-Nisa'a, 4:75)

   "But if they seek your help in religion, it is your duty to help them except against a people with whom you have a treaty of mutual alliance." (The Qur'aan, Al-Anfal, 8:72)

3. Defense of religion against triflers, and fighting against those who try to stand in the way of conveying the divine message and law of Islam, because Islam is a world call which is not limited to certain people. Every human being must have the chance to hear and be acquainted with Islam and its principles of good, justice, fraternity, love and equality, after which he can decide whether or not to embrace this religion. The Qur'aan says, (the meaning of which is translated as):

   "And fight them until there is no more persecution, and the religion will all be for Allah alone." (The Qur'aan, Al-Anfal, 8:39)

If the enemy stops fighting and offers peace, war must be stopped, it is forbidden to carry on fighting against them, Allah said, (the meaning of which is translated as):

"So if they withdraw from you and fight not against you and offer you peace, then Allah has opened no way for you against them." (The Qur'aan, An-Nisa'a, 4:90)

Other types of wars, such as expansionist wars leading to destruction, or wars for pompous show of power, are prohibited by Islam because fighting is permitted only for raising high the word of Allah, not for personal desires. The Qur'aan says, (the meaning of which is translated as):

"Be not as those who came forth from their dwellings boastfully and to be seen of men." (The Qur'aan, Al-Anfal, 8:47)

The Prophet, (pbuh) stated, (the meaning of which is translated as):

"One who fights to uphold the message of Allah, is the person who carries on Jihad (fighting) in the cause of Allah." (Bukhari & Muslim).

While Islam permits fighting in cases of necessity or emergency, it has prescribed rules and standards that control it. No enemy should be killed unless he has participated in or helped with the fight. As for old people, women, children, patients, those taking care of the sick and the wounded and devoted worshippers, they must not be killed. The wounded should not be killed, the dead should not be mutilated, their animals should not be slaughtered, their houses should not be demolished, their waters and wells should not be contaminated, and those who flee from battle should not be chased, because all this is part of corruption. The Qur'aan says, (the meaning of which is translated as):

"...and seek not corruption in the earth, Lo! Allah loves not those who cause corruption." (The Qur'aan, Al-Qasas, 28:77)

And Allah's Messenger, peace be upon him, said:

"Fight in the name of Allah, and in the cause of Allah, those who disbelieve in Allah. Fight, but never betray, mutilate, or kill a newborn." (Muslim)

Abu Bakr, the first Caliph after the blessed Prophet used to advise commanders of the Muslim troops when he sent them for battle as follows:

"Listen to these ten tips and learn them by heart: Don't betray, defraud (by stealing from the war booty), break your promise, mutilate, kill a little child, kill an old man or a woman, injure or burn palm trees, cut down a fruitful tree, slaughter a sheep or a cow or a camel except for eating. You will come across people who secluded themselves in hermitages, so leave them alone." (Tabari, Vol. 3)

In addition, war should be declared prior to starting the fight, so as to avoid deceit, betrayal and perfidy.

As for prisoners of war, Islam does not allow them to be tortured, scared humiliated, mutilated or starved to death. The Qur'aan says, (the meaning of which is translated as):

"And (they) feed with food, despite their love and desire for it, the needy wretch, the orphan and the prisoner, (saying): 'We feed you for the sake of Allah only. We wish for no reward nor thanks from you.'" (The Qur'aan, Ad-Dahr, 76:8-9)

The Muslim State after that may either set them free without ransom, or for ransom (a sum of money) or in exchange for Muslim prisoners of war. Allah said, (the meaning of which is translated as):

"Now when you meet in battle those who disbelieve, then it is smiting on the necks until, when you have routed them, then making fast of bonds: and afterwards either grace or ransom till the war lay down its burdens." (The Qur'aan, Muhammad, 47:4).

As for non-Muslims who are defeated in war and are living under Muslim protection, Muslims are required to keep their honor intact, their wealth and property secure, their houses and property from being demolished or vandalized. They must not be exposed to any acts of vengeance; it is required to improve their conditions, enjoin on them what is good and prohibit them from doing evil things, treat them equally and respect their beliefs. The Glorious Qur'aan states in this regard, (the meaning of which is translated as):

"Those (Muslim rulers) who, if We give them power in the land, establish prayer and pay the poor due and enjoin kindness and forbid inequity. And Allah's is the sequel of events." (The Qur'aan, Al-Hajj, 22:41)

A good example is the pledge given by 'Umar Ibn Al-Khattab to the people of Jerusalem when he conquered it, it read as follows:

"In the name of Allah, the All-Beneficent, the All-Merciful. This is the pledge of protection given by Allah's Servant, 'Umar Ibn Al-Khattab, Commander of the Faithful, to the people of Jerusalem: To safeguard them, their property, churches, crosses, etc., not to be coerced in matters of their religion, and not to cause damage to any of them..."

Has history witnessed better than such noble-mindedness, justice and tolerance extended from a conqueror to the conquered? 'Umar could have dictated whatever he willed on them, but – as always – he preferred justice and adhered to the dictates of divine Law enforcing it on all people equally.

A small amount of money is required of them, namely "the tribute" or Jizia, to be collected from those who choose to stick to their religion and not to embrace Islam. It is classified into three categories:

1. A sum of money taken from the rich, amounting to 48 dirhams[10] a year.
2. A sum taken from middle class people, such as traders and farmers, amounting to 24 dirhams a year.
3. A sum taken from workmen and craftsmen (who have jobs), amounting to 12 dirhams a year.

This tribute is generally paid for protection, care, and safeguarding them, their honor and wealth, and enjoying all rights enjoyed by the Muslim conquerors. Khalid Ibn Al-Waleed, in one of his treaties stated: *"I have covenanted with you for both tribute and protection. If we protect you we will receive the tribute; otherwise we will take nothing until we protect you."*[11]

---

[10] A dirham is a silver coin that weighs 2.979 grams.

[11] Al-Balazari's *History*.

This tax is not incumbent on all non-Muslim subjects. Poor and young people, women, monks in their hermitage, blind and disabled people are all exempted from the tax. Besides, the Muslim State is responsible for taking care of these people and providing them with their expenses from the Treasury. In a pledge given by the Muslim Leader Khalid Ibn Al-Waleed to people of Al-Hirah,[12] it was sated:

"Whatever old man who is unable to work or stricken with illness, or he becomes poor after affluence so that the followers of his religion give charity to him, he shall be relieved of the tribute and supported along with his family from the Treasury." (Abu Yusuf: Al-Kharaj)

Once 'Umar Ibn Al-khattab passed by an old Jewish man who was begging, when he asked about him and knew he used to pay the tribute tax he said to him;

"It's unfair to take the tax from you while young and then neglect you in old age."

Then he took him to his own house and gave him food and clothes. Later he instructed the Treasurer to look for such poor people and give them sufficient provisions for them and their families from the Treasury, for Allah says, (the meaning of which is translated as):

"The alms (of Zakat) are only for the poor and the needy..."

"The poor are the Muslims and the needy are the people of the Scriptures." (ibid)

The German woman researcher, Lise Lictenstadter, stated,

"In Persian and Roman territories, a choice was given to people. Not between the sword and Islam, but between Islam and the poll-tax or tribute (taken only from well-to-do people for their protection), the plan that was worthy of praise; it was adopted later in England during the rule of Queen Elizabeth." (Islam in the Modern Age, p. 67).

---

[12] The capital city of the Arab Lakhmi Kings. It was located between Najaf and Kufa in Iraq.

Non-Muslims in Muslim territories must be protected from oppression and injustice. Their rights must be respected and they should receive fair treatment. The Qur'aan says, (the meaning of which is translated as):

> *"Allah does not forbid you to deal justly with those who fought not against you on account of religion nor drove you out of your homes. Verily, Allah loves those who deal with equity." (The Qur'aan, Al-Mumtahana, 60:8)*

The Gracious Prophet, (pbuh) said:

> *"If a person wrongs, belittles, overburdens or robs a free non-Muslim under Muslim rule by force, I shall be his opponent on the Day of Judgement." (Abu Dawood)*

The Economic Aspect of Islam

Islam aims to erect a society free from excessively rich or poor people, because it seeks to establish social justice and honorable living for all its members. Allah, Glory to Him, tells us, (the meaning of which is translated as):

"Wealth and children are an ornament of life of the world."
(The Qur'aan, Al-Kahf, 18:46)

Since Islam considers money one of the indispensable necessities for individuals and groups, it has ordained a specific percentage, 2.5% called poor due or Zakat, to be taken from the funds of rich people after the elapse of one lunar year and given to poor people as explained before. It is one of the rights due to the poor and cannot be withheld from them.

This does not mean that Islam abolishes individual ownership and private business, in fact, it sanctions and respects them in terms of giving everyone his due. The Qur'aan has forbidden any aggression against the property of others by saying, (the meaning of which is translated as):

"And eat not up your property among yourselves in vanity."
(The Qur'aan, Al-Baqarah, 2:188)

Islam, therefore, has enacted Laws and regulations, the implementation of which is guaranteed by keenness on the attainment of honorable life for every member of the Muslim society. Such regulations include the following:

1. Usury has been forbidden because it exploits the efforts of others or taking their property unrightfully. Property is inviolable. The spread of usury will lead to the loss of kindness among people and the accumulation of wealth in the hands of a certain group of people. The Qur'aan addresses Muslims saying, (the meaning of which is translated as):

    "O you who believe! Be afraid of Allah and give up what remains (due to you) from usury, if you are (really) believers. And if you do not do it, then take a notice of war from Allah and His Messenger, but if you repent, you shall

have your capital sums (without interest). Wrong not, and you shall not be wronged." (The Qur'aan, Al-Baqarah, 2:278-279)

The Islamic Law prescribes that a grace period should preferably be granted to a debtor in case of insolvency if he really intends to pay back his debt, Allah said, (the meaning of which is translated as):

"And if the debtor is in a hard time, then grant him time till it is easy for him to repay." (The Qur'aan, Al-Baqarah, 2:280)

The Prophet, (pbuh) said:

"Whoever gives a grace period to one in debt, he will be deemed to have done an act of charity for each day."

2. Islam recommends reduction of debt in case of difficulty in repayment, Allah said, (the meaning of which is translated as):

"...but if you remit it by way of charity, that is better for you." (The Qur'aan, Al-Baqarah, 2:280)

3. It prohibits a person from entering into a transaction when his brother is already making a transaction, unless the latter gives permission, because this would lead to enmity and hatred among people. The Prophet, (pbuh) said:

"A person should not enter into a transaction when his brother is already making a transaction, and he should not make a proposal of marriage when his brother has already made a proposal, except when he gives permission." (Muslim)

4. Greed and hoarding of foodstuff are forbidden as this would lead to food shortage in the market and to inflated prices, which is harmful to both the rich and the poor. The Prophet, (pbuh) said:

"No one hoards but the sinner." (Muslim)

According to Abu Yusuf, the fellow scholar of Imam Abu Hanifah:

"If the hoarding of any goods proves to be harmful to the public, it would be considered a monopoly, even if it is gold

or silver. Whoever hoards it is deemed to have abused his right of ownership. The prevention of monopoly aims to protect people from harm, for people have different needs and monopoly causes hardship to people."

A ruler may force one who hoards a commodity to sell it at a reasonable profit, which is prejudicial neither to the seller nor the purchaser. If the monopolist refuses to sell at that profit, the ruler may confiscate the commodity and sell it at a reasonable price in order to stop the monopolists from hoarding.

5. It has prohibited unwarranted taxes as pointed out in the Prophet's Hadith:

"A taxman shall never be admitted into Paradise." (Abu Dawood)

An unwarranted tax is a sum of money collected from a trader to allow them to sell their goods or to import them into the country. This money is collected unlawfully and given also to those who are not entitled to it. All those who contribute to tax collection, including tax collectors, clerks, witnesses and receivers, come under the Prophet's saying:

"No flesh that grows from unlawful things shall be admitted into Paradise; Hell-fire shall have the best claim to them." (Imam Ahmad)

Unlawful things here include any unlawful amounts of money, food or drink.

6. It has forbidden hoarding up gold and silver (i.e.: money) and refraining from spending them on the welfare of both the individual and the society. The Qur'aan declares, (the meaning of which is translated as):

"They who hoard up gold and silver and spend it not in the way of Allah, unto them give tidings of painful doom." (The Qur'aan, At-Tauba, 9:34)

This is because money should be in current or general use so that the economy remains active and beneficial to all members of the society.

As Islam respects individual ownership, it imposes rights and duties associated with it. Such duties include the owner's duty to spend on himself and on those relatives supported by him, his duty towards the members of his society (including the payment of Zakat, almsgiving and kindness) and his duty toward his society collectively (including the construction... of schools, hospitals, orphanages, mosques and everything of use to the society). This will help prevent the accumulation of wealth in the hands of a limited number of people.

7. It has forbidden wine (alcoholic drinks) and gambling since they help squander human and financial resources and capabilities without benefiting either individuals or the society in general. Allah said, (the meaning of which is translated as):

   "Inded, intoxicants, gambling, idols, and divining arrows are only an infamy of Satan's handiwork. Leave it aside in order that you may succeed." (The Qur'aan Chapter Al-Ma'idah 5:90)

8. It has forbidden giving less in measure and weight. The Glorious Qur'aan says in this regard, (the meaning of which is translated as):

   "Woe to those who give less in measure and weight, Those who, when they have to receive by measure from men, demand full measure, and when they have to give by measure or weight to (other) men, give less than due." (The Qur'aan 83:1-3)

That is because it is a kind of stealth and deceit.

9. It has prohibited monopolizing public utilities, such as water and public pastures, and preventing people from benefiting by them. Allah's Messenger, (pbuh) said:

   "There are three persons whom Allah will not talk to, look at, or purify on the Day of Judgment, and they will suffer a painful punishment... and a man who refused to give excess water (to those who need it badly). On that day, Allah will say to him: 'Today I withhold from you my grace as you withheld what is in excess of your needs, though you are not its creator.'" (Bukhari & Muslim)

10. The Law of Inheritance: Islam has distributed inheritance among heirs according to nearness or distance of relationship and benefit to the deceased. Nobody has the

right to distribute inheritance as he wishes. One of the advantages of inheritance distribution is that it breaks up wealth or property, however large, into small amounts or estates, and precludes accumulation of wealth in the hands of a particular group of people.

11. Private and Public Social Security: Islam has prescribed the systems of endowments, which falls into two categories.

   A. Private or special endowment limited to the family or offspring of the initiator of the endowment with the aim of protecting them from want and begging. One of the conditions of validity of this type of endowment is to transfer its returns and benefit, when no more offspring exists, to welfare work and charitable purposes.

   B. Public or general charitable endowment, which aims to use the income of endowed property, or the property itself, for the sake of welfare and benevolence, including the construction of hospitals, schools, roads, public libraries, mosques, social welfare houses for orphans, and old people. All of this is in the interest of the whole society.

12. Islam has forbidden all that comes under the Quranic verse:

   "O you who believe! Eat not up your wealth among yourselves in vanity." (The Qur'aan, An-Nisa'a, 4:29)

This includes:

• Usurpation, which involves wronging others and perverting society; The Prophet, (pbuh) said:

"Whoever usurps a Muslim's property through a false oath, Allah will make Hell his abode and forbid him from Paradise."

One man asked: *"Even if it were the twig of a bush, O Messenger of Allah?"* The Prophet answered,

"Even if it were the twig of a bush." (Muslim)

• Robbery, The Glorious Qur'aan states, (the meaning of which is translated as):

"As for the thief, both male and female, cut off their hands. It is the reward of their own deeds: an exemplary punishment from Allah." (The Qur'aan, Al-Ma'idah, 5:38)

- Deceit and Cheating, Allah's Messenger, (pbuh) said:

  "One who cheats is not one of us." (Muslim)

- Bribery, the Qur'aan says, (the meaning of which is translated as):

"And eat not up your property among yourselves in vanity, nor seek by it to gain the hearing of the judges that you may knowingly devour a portion of the property of others wrongfully." (The Qur'aan, Al-Baqarah, 2:188)

Prophet Muhammad, (pbuh) said in this connection:

"May Allah curse the briber, the one bribed, and the one who goes between them." (Ibn Hibban).

The one bribed, by giving a bribe, helps to spread this evil in society. By accepting a bribe, the one doing the bribing takes what is not his, unrightfully, and commits a breach of trust for he takes a price for a duty above the designated salary or wages. The one who goes between the giver and receiver of a bribe helps to promote this sin and accepts unlawful money.

- A man should not buy in opposition to his brother unless the latter gives him permission. The Prophet, (pbuh) said, (the meaning of which is translated as):

"Do not forsake one another, nor buy in opposition to each other." (Muslim)

The Social Aspect of Islam

Islamic Laws have regulated the mutual rights and duties of the members of society in order to ensure social stability. Such rights and duties are either special or general. Special rights and duties or obligations include:

- People's Obligations Towards the Ruler:

It is stated in the Noble Qur'aan, (the meaning of which is translated as):

"O you who believe! Obey Allah and obey the Messenger (Muhammad), and those of you who are in authority." (The Qur'aan, An-Nisa'a, 4:59)

These obligations are as follows:

- To obey the ruler unless his orders are in conflict with Islam. This is in keeping with the Prophet's (pbuh) Hadith:

"Listen and obey, even if an Abyssinian slave is appointed as your leader, as long as he implements Allah's Book (i.e.:The Qur'aan) among you." (Narrated by the Major Hadith Imams, except Bukhari).

Thus, obedience to the ruler, if he orders no sin, is part of obedience to Allah, hence disobedience to him, in this context, implies disobedience to Allah.

- To extend sincere advice to the ruler, gently and leniently, on things that are helpful to him and are in the interest of his subjects. Allah, glory to Him, instructed Moses and his brother Aaron, on sending them to Pharaoh to preach the true religion to him:

"And speak to him mildly, perhaps he may accept admonition or fear (Allah." (The Qur'aan, Ta-Ha, 20:44).

- To stand up for him in times of adversity or crises and not to rise against him or let him down, even though he does not pledge allegiance to him. According to the Prophet's:

"If someone comes, while you are united under one leader, and he wants to stir up discord among you or to disrupt your unity, just kill him." (Muslim)

- The Ruler's Obligations towards the Ruled People's rights or the ruler's obligations toward them can be summed up by five items:

1. Absolute justice which is realized by giving everyone higher due. So a ruler is required to be fair in protecting others' rights. Performing his duties, distribution or allocation of responsibilities, and implementation or rules and decisions. All people are equal before him the ruler. If a person or group should be favored more than others, the Prophet (pbuh) said:

> *"The nearest to Allah and most favored by Him is the fair ruler and the worst is a tyrant and the most disliked by Him is the unfair one."* *(Tirmidhi)*

2. He should consult them regarding all affairs pertaining to their political, social and economic interests (consultation is limited to those matters for which there is no explicit text from the Qur'aan or Sunnah), allows them the chance to give their views and express themselves freely, and accept such views if they prove to be in the public interest. When the Prophet, in the battle of Badr, stopped at the nearest spring of Badr, one of his companions asked him, *"Has Allah inspired you to choose this very spot or is it strategy of war?"* The Prophet replied, *"It is the strategy of war."* The companion said, *"This place is no good, let us go and camp on the well nearest to the enemy and make a basin full of water, then destroy all the wells so that the enemy should be deprived of water."* The Prophet approved of his plan and agreed to carry it out.

3. The Islamic Law, must be the source of the ruler's decisions and constitution. This leaves no way for personal whims or wanton decisions that may hit or miss the mark. 'Umar Ibn Al-Khattab, may Allah be pleased with him, after assuming the Caliphate, said to Abu Maryam Al-Saluli, who had killed his brother Zaid Ibn Al-Khattab (before he embraced Islam). *"By Allah, I won't like you until the earth likes blood."* Al-Saluli asked: *"Will this deprive me of any of my rights?"* 'Umar replied: *"No"* The man said: *"No harm, only women will be unhappy if they are not liked."*

4. He should not conceal himself from his people or lock his doors in their faces, nor should he look down upon them and place between himself and his subjects mediators who allow some people in and prevent others. The Gracious Prophet, (pbuh) said:

"Whoever is appointed, by Allah's favor, as ruler or governor, then keeps himself absent from them, thereby ignoring their needs and poverty, Allah will ignore his needs and destitution on the Day of Judgment." (Abu Dawood and Tirmidhi)

5. He should be merciful to his subjects. He should not assign to them unbearable or unaffordable tasks or constrict their way of living. Also he should treat the elderly as parents, the young as sons or daughters and those his own age as his brothers. Thus he respects his parents, shows mercy to his children and respects his brothers. The Glorious Qur'aan says, (the meaning of which is translated as):

"And by the Mercy of Allah, you dealt with them gently. And had you been severe and harsh hearted, they would have broken away from about you, so pass over (their faults), and ask (Allah's) forgiveness for them; and consult them in the affairs." (The Qur'aan, Chapter Ali 'Imran, 3:159)

The Prophet (pbuh) said, (the meaning of which is translated as):

"Allah shows His mercy to those who are merciful. Show mercy to those living on earth, and Allah will give you His mercy." (Abu Dawood and Tirmidhi)

'Umar Ibn Al-Khattab indicated the importance of this by saying:

"By Allah, if a mule tripped over and fell in Iraq, I would be afraid that Allah will ask me why I did not level the road for it."

A Muslim ruler must be as described in a letter which Imam Al-Hassan Al-Basri sent to 'Umar Ibn 'Abdul-'Aziz, may Allah's mercy be on him, in which he said:

"O Commander of the Faithful, be informed that Allah has made the fair ruler a prop for supporting what is tilted (not upright), a restraint on oppressors, a reformation of perverted people, strength for the weak, justice to the oppressed, and a refuge for the afflicted.

A fair ruler, O Commander of the Faithful, is like a shepherd who is kind to his camels, so he looks for the best pasture and drives them away from the areas of danger, wild animals and hot or cold weather. The just ruler, O Commander of the Faithful, is like a caring father who toils for the sake of his children, educates them as they grow up, supports them and keeps for them what he leaves to them after his death.

O Commander of the Faithful, a just ruler is like an affectionate mother who has loving care for her son. She bore him with hardship. She cared for him when he was a little child; she sat up late with him when he stayed awake at night, and became calm when he was peaceful, at times feeding him, and at other times weaning him, feeling happy about his good health and unhappy about his complaints.

O Commander of the Faithful, a just ruler is the guardian of orphans and a sponsor of the needy: he cares for the young and provides for the old.

A just ruler, O Commander of the Faithful, is like a heart within the ribs: when the heart is healthy the ribs become healthy, but when it is sick they grow unhealthy.
A just ruler, O Commander of the Faithful, stands between Allah and His servants: He hears the word of Allah and conveys it to them, looks forward to Allah (with his heart) and makes them look forward to Him, submits his will to his Lord and leads them to Him.

O Commander of the Faithful, don't be, in what Allah has bestowed upon you, like a slave who was entrusted by his master with his wealth and family, but he wasted the master's wealth and made his children homeless and destitute.

As you know, Prince of the Faithful, Allah has prescribed punishments (stipulated in the Qur'aan) to deter his servants from deadly sins and evils, what if the one in charge of such punishments commits such sins? Allah has also stipulated retaliation to protect the lives of the people, what then if the one who is in charge of retaliation commits murder?

O Commander of the Faithful, recall death and the Hereafter, and the futility of your supporters and followers in the face of death, so get ready for it and the horrors that follow.

O Commander of the Faithful! You should know that, apart from your present residence, there is still another one where your sleep will last long, and your friends will part company with you and leave you alone at the bottom of that place. Therefore, provide yourself with what keeps you company "on the days when a man flees from his brother, and his mother and his father, and his wife and his children?"[13] *Remember also the time, "when the contents of the graves are poured fourth: and the secrets of the breasts are made known."*[14] *Thus secrets are out, and there is "a book... that leaves not a small thing but has counted it." Now there is still time for you before death comes and hopes are shattered and lost.*

O Commander of the Faithful! Do not judge between them in the way of ignorant people. Do not lead them in the way of the wrong-doers. Do not give proud people power over feeble ones, as they observe towards a believer neither pact nor honor, so that you should not bear the burdens of other sins besides yours. Do not be deceived by those who enjoy those things that lead to your misery, and devour the good things while depriving you of the good things of the Hereafter. Do not think of your power today; think of it tomorrow when you become the captive of death. Then stand on the Day of Judgment before Almighty Allah in the presence of an assembly of angels, prophets and messengers, when "faces humble themselves before the Living and Eternal" Allah, glory be to Him.

O Commander of the Faithful! I have not attained with my advice the level of wise preachers or men or reason and wisdom before me; but I have done my best to be sincere in my advice to you. So take my message to you as a medicine

---

[13] Quoted from the Qur'an 80:34-36

[14] Qur'an 100:9-10

given by a loving person to his favorite friend, though it has bitter taste, in the hope of his cure.

Peace, mercy and blessings of Allah be upon you."

❖ **Parents' Rights**

They have a claim on our obedience to them (unless a sin is involved) and responding to their orders. We should extend our kindness and generosity to them, and provide them with their necessities, including food, drink, clothes and accommodation. We are required to speak to them leniently and humbly, to serve them patiently, and to respect their feelings, no words should be addressed to them that hurt their feelings. The Qur'aan recommends in this respect by saying, (the meaning of which is translated as):

"And your Lord has decreed that you worship none but Him, and that you be dutiful to your parents. If one of them or both of them attain old age in your life, say not to them a word of disrespect, nor shout at them but address them in terms of honor. And lower unto them the wing of submission and humility through mercy, and Say: 'My Lord! Bestow on them your Mercy as they did bring me up when I was young.'" (The Qur'aan, Bani Israil, 17:23-24)

The great Prophet, (pbuh) said:

"Allah's pleasure originates from parents' pleasure, and His wrath originates from parents' anger." (Tirmidhi)

The aforesaid rights are due to parents even if they were non-Muslims in the light of Ayesha's tradition in which she said:

"My mother visited me when she was an idolater. I inquired with Allah's Messenger, peace be upon him, saying: 'O Messenger of Allah! My mother has visited me willingly. Shall I receive her?' He answered: 'Yes, receive and honor her.'" (Bukhari & Muslim)

The mother is given priority over the father in matters of kind treatment and good companionship. This is understood from the following tradition:

"A man came to Allah's Messenger, peace be upon him, and asked: 'O Messenger of Allah, which person of all the people

is best entitled to my kind treatment and companionship?'
He answered: 'Your mother', The man asked: 'And then?'
He said: 'Your mother', and after her? He said: 'Your
mother', and after her? The Prophet, peace be upon him,
said: 'Your father'".

The Prophet (pbuh) accorded the mother three rights and the father one right, because the former bears hardships and suffering that the latter cannot bear. As described in the Noble Qur'aan, (the meaning of which is translated as):

"His mother bears him with hardship, and gives him birth
with hardship." (The Qur'aan, Al-Ahqaf, 46:15)

She suffers from hardship when she bears him in her womb, when she gives birth to him, and when she feeds and cares for him after delivery.

❖ **A Wife's Obligations towards her Husband**:

1. To acknowledge her husband's authority and management of the family's affairs in the best interest of the family. However, this authority is not an absolute authority or superiority. The Quran says, (the meaning of which is translated as):

"Men are in charge of women, because Allah has made the
one of them to excel the other, and because they spend of
their property (for the support of women)." (The Qur'aan,
An-Nisa'a, 4:34)

That is because men generally use their minds in dealing with events, in contrast to women whose conduct are dominated by emotions.

2. To obey him unless his orders or requests are in conflict with Allah's commands. When the Prophet (pbuh) was asked by Ayesha about the one who has the greatest claim on a woman's obedience, he (pbuh) replied: *"Her husband."* When asked who has the greatest claim on a man's obedience and kindness, he replied: *"His mother."* (Al-Hakim)

3. She should not refuse to go with her husband when he calls her to bed. The Prophet (pbuh) said:

"If a man calls his wife to his bed and she refuses, and he spends the night in anger with her, the angels will keep cursing her till the morning." (Bukhari & Muslim)

4. She should not request things that are unaffordable by her husband. It is her duty to protect his wealth, children and reputation, not to go out of his house without his permission; and not to allow into his house anyone whom he dislikes. The Prophet (pbuh) said:

"The best of women is the one who pleases her husband when he looks at her, obeys him if he orders her, and preserves herself (her chastity) and his property in his absence." (Tabarani).

Early Muslims used to put such instructions into effect. A woman gave this piece of advice to her daughter on her wedding day:

"My daughter, you have parted your home where you have grown up, to a man you are not familiar with. So be his maid and he will be your slave. Observe for him ten qualities, and he will be a treasure for you: contentment, obedience, taking care of your beauty and pleasant smell, taking heed of the time of his sleep and meals, taking care of his wealth and children, refraining from disobedience to him, and keeping his secrets. Don't show pleasure with him when he is worried or grief when he is pleased."

❖ **A Husband's Obligations towards his Wife**

1. The Dowry

A woman has a right to a dowry, which should be stated when concluding the marriage contract. It is an essential part of the marriage contract and cannot be conceded or given away by the wife until the contract has been concluded. The Qur'aan states, (the meaning of which is translated as):

"And give unto the woman their bridal gift with a good heart; but if they of their own accord remit unto you a part thereof, then you are welcome to consume it without any harm." The Qur'aan, An-Nisa'a, 4:4).

2. Justice and Equality

If a man has more than one wife, he is required to be fair in their treatment, including food, drink, dress, residence and stay, in the light of the Prophet's (pbuh)tradition:

"If a man has two wives yet does not treat them equally, he will come dragging one side on the Day of Judgment." (Tirmidhi).

3. Spending on his Wife and Children

A husband is required to provide appropriate residence, living requirements, as well as money within his means. The Qur'aan says, (the meaning of which is translated as):

"Let the rich man spend according to his means; and the man whose resources are restricted, let him spend according to what Allah has given him. Allah puts no burden on any person beyond what He has given him." (The Qur'aan, At-Talaq, 65:7)

4. Overnight Stay and Sexual Intercourse

It is one of the husbands' important obligations. As a wife, she is in need of a loving heart and a husband who plays with her, caresses her and satisfies her desire to protect her from undesired consequences.

5. Keeping her Secrets

He should keep private (intimate) relationship secrets, and refrain from exposing her secrets, shortcomings and other things he notices or hears from her. The Gracious Prophet (pbuh) said:

"The worst of people before Allah on the Day of Judgment, is the man who goes with his wife, or she with him, then one of them divulges the secrets of the other." (Muslim)

6. Good Treatment

A husband should treat his wife with kindness. He should be patient with her and tolerate her slips and nuisances. Besides, he should consult her in mutual everyday matters, provide her with the means of happiness and comfort by joking and playing with her.

7. Modesty and its Preservation

He protects her from incidents of evil and corruption. In this regard, Allah, glory to Him, orders us by saying, (the meaning of which is translated as):

"O you who believe! Protect yourselves and your families against a Fire (Hell) whose fuel is men and stones." (The Qur'aan, At-Tahrim, 66:6)

8. Preserving her Money or Property

He should not take anything that belongs to her unless she gives him permission, nor should any of her property be disposed of without her approval.

❖ Rights of Relatives

Islam has urged well to do people to help their relatives by complying with their needs, inquiring about their conditions, treating them with kindness and sympathy and sharing their joys and sorrows. The Qur'aan says, (the meaning of which is translated as):

> "And fear Allah through Whom you demand (your mutual rights), and do not cut the relations of the wombs (kinship)." (The Qur'aan, An-Nisa'a, 4:1)

Islam has urged good treatment of one's close relatives even if they do not treat him kindly, forgiving them even if they wrong him, and seeking their friendship even if they are unfriendly with him. The Noble Prophet (pbuh) said:

> "To be kind to your close relatives in the full meaning of the word, it is not sufficient to match them in kindness; but to be kind to them when they cut relation with you." (Bukhari)

Islam has also warned against cutting the relations of kinship and considered it one of the major sins. In the Qur'aan it is stated, (the meaning of which is translated as):

> "Would you then, if you were given the authority, do mischief in the land, and sever your ties of kinship?" (The Qur'aan, Muhammad, 47:22)

❖ Rights of Children

Children have the right to safeguard their lives and have appropriate names. This is made clear in the Prophet's (pbuh) tradition:

> "You will be called by your given names and fathers' names, so have beautiful names." (Imam Ahmed)

We should also take care of them, provide their needs, give them a proper education and teach them good manners. We should also prevent them from bad speech or behavior. The Noble Prophet (pbuh) said:

"It suffices a man to be a sinner that he ruins him whom he supports." *(Abu Dawood & Nas'e)*

He (pbuh) also said, (the meaning of which is translated as):

"All of you hold a responsibility over someone, and you will be questioned about your responsibility." *(Bukhari & Muslim)*

Children should be treated equally and no discrimination in gifts or kind treatment should be made between them. This is because such discrimination would cause undutiful behavior and hatred. Once a man came to Allah's Messenger (pbuh) to make him a witness to a gift he intended to give one of his children. The Prophet, however, asked him : *"Have you made a similar gifts to each of your children?"* He said no, whereupon the Prophet said: *"Then make someone else a witness to this, for I do not wan to be a witness to an injustice. Fear Allah and be fair to your children."* (Bukhari & Muslim)

❖ Rights of Neighbors

Islam has enjoyed kindness to neighbors and refrain from causing them any physical or psychological inconvenience, like raising one's voice, offending his sight with disliked things or his nose with harmful smell. Allah, glory to Him, says, (the meaning of which is translated as):

"And worship Allah. Ascribe nothing as partner unto Him. (Show) kindness unto parents, and unto near kindred, and orphans, and the needy, and unto the neighbor who is of kin (unto you) and the neighbor who is not of kin, and the fellow traveler and the wayfarer and (the captives) whom your right hand possess. Lo! Allah loves not such as are proud and boastful." *(The Qur'aan, An-Nisa'a, 4:36)*

In another tradition, the Prophet (pbuh) states a neighbor's rights:

"Do you know what a neighbor's rights are? If he asks you for help, you should provide help for him, if he falls ill you should visit him, if something good happens to him you should congratulate him, if something bad happens to him you should console him; if he dies you should participate in his funeral procession. You should not raise your building so high that you obstruct the passage of wind to him unless he

gives his permission. You should not hurt him with the smell of your cooking pot unless you send him some of the food. If you buy fruit send him some as a gift, otherwise you have to bring it into your house secretly and not allow your children to take it out to vex his children with it." (Al-Khara'iti)

A Muslim should bear the trouble caused by his neighbor and extend kindness to him. One man came to 'Abdullah Ibn 'Abbas and said to him: A neighbor of mine causes me a lot of trouble, insults me and causes me inconvenience. Ibn 'Abbass replied: *"If he disobeys Allah (by hurting you), Obey Allah (by being kind to him)."* (Imam Ghazali, Ihyaa Ulum-ud-Din, Vol. 2, p.212)

He should respect his neighbor, even if he tries to places a beam on his wall he should not prevent him, as understood from the Prophet's (pbuh) words:

"Let not a neighbor forbid his immediate neighbor from placing his beam on his wall." (Bukhari & Muslim)

He should not sell or lease a property that is adjacent to him before he offers it to him or seeks his advice about that. This is based on the Prophet's (pbuh) tradition:

"If one has a neighbor or partner in a farm or garden, let him not sell it until he offers him to purchase it first." (Al-Hakim)

There are three kinds of neighbors:

1. A neighbor who is a relative. He has three rights: as a relative, as a neighbor and as a Muslim.
2. A Muslim neighbor. He has two rights: as a neighbor and as a Muslim.
3. A non-Muslim neighbor. He has one right, as a neighbor.

'Abdullah Ibn 'Umar had a sheep slaughtered, then asked his family: Have you sent our Jewish neighbor some of it as present? I heard Allah's Messenger (pbuh) say, (the meaning of which is translated as):

"Gabriel kept exhorting me about (obligations towards) the neighbor so much that I thought that he would include him among the heirs." (Tirmidhi & Abu Dawood)

❖ Rights of Friends and Companions

Islam has taken great care of friends' rights and prescribed certain rights that should be fulfilled for a friend, such as kind treatment and sincere advice. The Prophet (pbuh) said:

"The best friend before of Allah is the one who is best to his companion, and the best neighbor before Allah is he who behaves best towards his neighbors." (Tirmidhi)

❖ Rights of Guests

Guests have a right to hospitality. This is based on the Noble Prophet's (pbuh) following tradition:

"One who believes in Allah and the Day of Judgment should honor his guest according to his right." He was asked: "O Messenger of Allah! What is his right?" He said: "A day and night (of provisions) or hospitality for three days. Thereafter it is an act of charity." (Bukhari & Muslim).

A guest, however, should take the conditions of his host into consideration, not burdening him with what he cannot afford. The Prophet (pbuh) said:

"It is lawful for a Muslim to stay so long with his brother (as a guest) as to not involve himself in sin" He was asked as to how he could be involved in sin? He answered: "By prolonging his stay with his host when he has nothing (left in his house) to entertain him with" (Muslim).

Imam Ghazali, in his book, "Ihyaa Ulum-ud-Din" (the Revival of Religious Sciences), wrote about Prophet Muhammad (pbuh) who is an example to all Muslims:

"The Prophet used to honor his guests, he even spread his garment for a non-relative guest to sit on it. He used to offer his guest his own cushion and insist until the latter would accept it from him. No one came to him as a guest but thought that he was the most generous of people. He gave each one of his companions sitting with him his due portion of his attention. He directed his listening, talking, looking and attention to all his companions. His meetings were characterized by modesty, humbleness and honesty. He used

to call his companions by their favorite nickname to honor them. He was the farthest from being angry and the easiest to be content."

❖ **General Rights and Obligations**

Islam requires a Muslim to take care of his Muslim brothers by extending help to them and trying to improve their conditions wherever they are. This is stressed by the following Hadith:

"Muslims, in their mutual love, kindness and compassion, are like one body: If one of its parts is in agony, the entire body feels the pain both in sleeplessness and fever." (Bukhari & Muslim).

Another Hadith says:

"The bonds of brotherhood between two Muslims are like parts of a house, one part strengthens and supports the other." He crossed the fingers of one hand between those of the other. (Bukhari & Muslim)

Another Hadith says:

"None of you is a believer until he loves for his brother what he loves for himself." (Bukhari)

In the field of labor, for example, Islam has enacted rules and criteria that determine the employer-employee relationship.

❖ **Labor's Rights**

The employer – labor relationship must be based on brotherhood and equality in human dignity. Prophet Muhammad (pbuh) said:

"Your servants are your brothers whom Allah the Most High has placed under your authority. Therefore, a person who has a brother under his authority, should feed him out of that which he eats himself. He should dress him with the same kind of clothes he wears. He should not assign work to him that is beyond his capacity, and if you do so, then help him in his work." (Bukhari)

Islam has preserved the workman's honor and dignity. The Prophet (pbuh) said:

"The best gain is that of the workman who works to earn his living if he sticks to honesty." (Ahmad)

It ordained that workman's wages should be made clear before he commences his work, for the Prophet, peace be upon him, required the employer to make the workman's wage clear before he hires him. (Ahmad)

It confirmed the workman's right to his wages. The Prophet (pbuh) said that Allah said:

"There are three for who I will be an adversary on the Day of Judgment: The person who makes a promise with an oath in My name and then breaks it. The person who sells a free man as a slave and spends the price; And the person who engages a workman and having taken full work from him fails to pay him his dues." (Bukhari)

It is required that he should be given his wages immediately after he completed his work. The Prophet (pbuh) said:

"Give a worker his wages before his sweat dries." (Ibn Majah)

It is also required for employers not to assign work that is beyond the worker's ability. If they assign such heavy work they should help them materially by increasing their wages, or physically by helping them with their work. The Prophet (pbuh) said:

"Do not give them work that is beyond their capacity and if you do so, then help them with their work." (Bukhari)

❖ **The Employers Rights**

As Islam required the employer to care for his employee's rights, it requires the employees, in return, to observe the employer's rights by carrying out their work in the best manner. The Prophet (pbuh) said:

"Allah likes, if one of you performs a portion of work, that he should do it well."

This means that a Muslim who is entrusted with a job should do it well as this is a means for gaining favor with his Almighty Lord.

Moral Aspects of Islam

In Islam manners are of different categories. In summary, they are either virtuous or evil. Virtuous manners are all good acts and sayings, such as honesty, telling the truth, charity, cooperation and modesty. Whereas evil ones are all harmful acts and sayings, such as dishonesty, telling lies, injustices, cruelty and hatred.

The Qur'aan has summed up good manners in the following verse, (the meaning of which is translated as):

"Keep to forgiveness (O Muhammad), and enjoin kindness, and turn away from the ignorant." (The Qur'aan, Al-A'raf, 7:199)

The Prophet Muhammad (pbuh) has stated the objective of his mission:

"I have been sent to raise good morals to perfection." (Bukhari)

Examples of Some Prohibited Acts

- Islam has forbidden polytheism, meaning associating partners to Allah. The Qur'aan says, (the meaning of which is translated as):

"Lo! Allah pardons not that partners should be ascribed unto Him. He pardons besides that whom He wills." (The Qur'aan, An-Nisa'a, 4:116)

It has forbidden all forms of magic. The Prophet (pbuh) said:

"Avoid the seven destructive sins." The companions asked: "O Messenger of Allah! What are these things? He answered: "Associating partners with Allah; magic; unwarranted killing of person whose life has been made sacred by Allah; usury; consuming the property of an orphan; fleeing in battle; and slandering chaste, innocent, believing women." (Bukhari & Muslim)

- It has forbidden injustice and oppression, which generally denote wronging others by words or deeds or failing to give others their due rights. The Noble Qur'aan says, (the meaning of which is translated as):

"The way (of blame) is only against those who oppress mankind, and wrongfully rebel in the earth. For such there is a painful doom." (The Qur'aan, Ash-Shura, 42:42)

It also says, (the meaning of which is translated as):

"Say: 'My Lord forbids only indecencies, such of them as are apparent and hidden and tyranny without right." The Qur'aan, Al-A'raf, 7:33)

The Prophet (pbuh) said:

"Allah the Most High has revealed to me that you should be humble, so that nobody oppresses, or holds himself above others." (Muslim)

In another tradition, the Prophet (pbuh) said:

"Allah admonishes you: 'O my servants, I have prohibited oppression on Myself and I have forbidden it among you. So do not wrong anyone." (Muslim)

This does not imply being content with humiliation, for Islam enjoined repressing injustice and preventing aggression. The Glorious Qur'aan says, (the meaning of which is translated as):

"And one who assaults you, assault him in like manner as he assaulted you." (The Qur'aan, Al-Baqarah, 2:194)

It also enjoined helping the victims of injustice even if they belonged to a different religion. The Noble Qur'aan said, (the meaning of which is translated as):

"And if one of the idolaters seeks your protection then protect him so that he may hear the Word of Allah, and afterward convey him to his place of safety." (The Qur'aan, At-Tauba, 9:6)

That is because Islam does not permit people to be deprived of their rights, their freedom, or for their feelings to be hurt, even if they are not Muslims.

It also enjoins this on both the oppressor and the oppressed. The Prophet (pbuh) said:

"Help your brother whether he is an oppressor or an oppressed person." A companion asked: "Messenger of Allah I will help him if he is an oppressed person, but please tell me how I am to help him if he happens to be an oppressor." The Prophet answered:"Prevent him from oppressing others. Because preventing him from committing aggression is a form of help for him." (Bukhari)

- It has prohibited slaying the life which Allah has forbidden except with due right. The Noble Qur'aan says, (the meaning of which is translated as):

"Whoever intentionally kills a believer, his recompense is Hell forever. Allah is wrath against him and He has cursed him and prepared for him an awful doom" (The Qur'aan, An-Nisa'a, 4:93)

The Qur'aan also says, (the meaning of which is translated as):

"For that cause We decreed upon the children of Israel that whosoever kills a soul for other than (retalitation for) unless for a soul or (to cause) corruption in the earth, it shall be as if he had killed all mankind. And whosoever saves the life of one, it shall be as if he saved the life of all mankind." (The Qur'aan, Al-Ma'idah, 5:32)

The Prophet (pbuh) said, (the meaning of which is translated as):

"A Muslim remains enjoying the safety and protection of his religion, so long as he does not commit an unlawful murder." (Bukhari)

Exempt from this threat are those who kill or are killed in self-defense, or defense of his property, or honor. Moreover, there is no difference whether the killed person is a Muslim or non-Muslim who are entitled to protection by the Muslim State. The Prophet (pbuh) said:

"Whoever killed a person with whom is a treaty, he shall not smell the smell of Paradise though its smell is perceived from a distance of forty years." (Bukhari)

- Islam has prohibited severing family ties and deserting relatives. Allah, the Most High, says, (the meaning of which is translated as):

"Would you then, if you were given the authority, do mischief in the land and sever your ties of kinship? Such are they whom Allah has cursed, so that He has made them deaf and blinded their sight." (The Qur'aan, Muhammad, 47:22-23)

The Prophet (pbuh) said:

"No one who severs the ties of kinship shall be admitted into Paradise." (Bukhari & Muslim)

Severing family ties includes failing to visit ones relatives in order to be aware of their condition. It also includes treating them in a degrading manner, and neglecting to help the poor and weak among them if one is affluent. This is because charity to the poor (if not a relative) is mere charity, but if its is a relative, then it will be considered both charity and a means of nurturing the ties of kinship. If one is without wealth to give, he can nurture the ties of kinship by greeting them, inquiring about their condition, and meeting them with gentle words and a cheerful smile. The Prophet (pbuh) encouraged good family relations saying:

"Nurture the ties of kinship with your relatives by greeting them with the greeting of peace."

- Islam has prohibited disobedience and unkindness to parents. The Qur'aan has stated, (the meaning of which is translated as):

"And your Lord has decreed that you worship none but Him, and that you be dutiful to your parents. If one of them or both of them attain old age in your life, say not to them a word of disrespect, nor shout at them but address them in terms of honor. And lower unto them the wing of submission and humility through mercy, and Say: 'My Lord! Bestow on them Your Mercy as they did bring me up when I was young.'" (The Qur'aan, Bani Israil, 17:23-24)

The Great Prophet Muhammad (pbuh) said, (the meaning of which is translated as):

"Allah's pleasure is based on parents' pleasure, and His wrath is based on their wrath." (Tirmidhi)

When asked about the definition of disobedience to parents, Ka'ab Al-Ahbar replied:

"It means that if one's parents take an oath he does not make good on their oath; if they order him he does not obey them; if they ask him for something he does not give them; and if they trust him he betrays their trust."

- Islam has forbidden fornication and all things and practices that lead to it. The Qur'aan says, (the meaning of which is translated as):

"And come not near to unlawful sexual intercourse. Verily, it is an abomination and an evil way." (The Qur'aan, Bani Israil, 17:32)

The Prophet (pbuh) said:

"There is no sin after polytheism worse than a man placing his sperm into an unlawful vulva." (Ahmad).

The Glorious Qur'aan mentioned a fornicator's punishment, (the meaning of which is translated as):

"The woman and the man guilty of illegal sexual intercourse, flog each of them with a hundred stripes. Let not pity withhold you in their case, in a punishment prescribed by Allah, if you believe in Allah and the Last Day. And let a party of the believers witness their punishment." (The Qur'aan, An-Nur, 24:2)

This punishment is for persons who were never married that commit the above crime. If persons married or previously married commit it, then the punishment is to stone them to death.

To put such punishment into effect, either of two prerequisites is a must:

1. Confession by both the man and woman who have committed this crime.

2. Four witnesses who are able to describe the event in the most minute of details, such that it proves the crime beyond all doubt.

This is, in fact, possible only when the two adulterers commit their crime in public and are witnessed the four witnesses, which is rare or even impossible. The history of Islam has witnessed only two or three events in which the punishment was carried out based on confession and only after those who committed adultery or fornication insisted on execution of the ordained punishment. Such punishment demonstrates the gravity of the committed sin and aims to preserve against the degradation of honor, to protect the people and their morals from corruption, the society from disintegration and disease, and the lineage from impurity and confusion in matters of inheritance and marriage. Allah's Messenger (pbuh) said:

"If the sin of adultery spreads among people in public, plague and other new diseases will also spread among them." (Ibn Majah)

The most abominable form of this sin is incest. One tradition related by Al-Hakim states:

"Whoever commits incest, kill him."

• Islam has forbidden sodomy. The Qur'aan tells us about the people of Lot, (the meaning of which is translated as):

"So when Our Commandment came, We turned (the towns of Sodom in Palestine) upside down, and rained on them stones of baked clay, in a well-arranged manner one after another; Marked from your Lord; and they are not ever far from the evil-doers.(The Qur'aan, Hud, 11:82-83)

The above suggests that whoever behaves like the people of Lot should beware lest he be struck with the same punishment. The Prophet (pbuh) said:

"Four person expose themselves to the wrath of Allah every morning and evening." When he was asked about them he answered:"Men who imitate women, women who imitate men, those who have sexual intercourse with animals and those who commit sodomy." (Tabarani)

Islam has forbidden devouring the property of orphans, as this involves wasting the rights of the weak. Allah said, (the meaning of which is translated as):

"Those who unjustly eat up the property of orphans, eat up a fires to their own bodies; they will soon be enduring a blazing fire!" (The Qur'aan, An-Nisa'a, 4:10)

An exception to this is the case of a poor guardian of an orphan. He is permitted to take a reasonable percentage or portion for his supervision, care, and services including feeding, clothing, and the investment of property in the best interest of the orphan. The Glorious Qur'aan states, (the meaning of which is translated as):

"And whoever (among guardians) is rich, he should take no wages, but if he is poor, let him have for himself what is just and reasonable." (The Qur'aan, An-Nisa'a, 4:6)

The Prophet (pbuh) recommended us to take care of orphans and treat them kindly, He (pbuh) said:

"I and the guardian of an orphan are like these."

He pointed his forefinger and middle finger. (Bukhari)

He also said:

"If a person takes a Muslim orphan and supports him until he grows up and is able to support himself, he will become worthy of entering Paradise, unless he commits an unforgivable sin." (Tirmidhi)

- Islam has forbidden the ruler to wrong or cheat his people. The Qur'aan says, (the meaning of which is translated as):

"Consider not that Allah is unaware of what the wrongdoers do, but He gives them respite up to a Day when the eyes will stare in horror. (They will be) hastening forward with necks outstretched, their heads raised up (towards the sky), their gaze returning not towards them and their hearts empty (from thinking because of extreme fear)." (The Qur'aan, Ibrahim, 14:42-43)

The Prophet (pbuh) said:

"If a ruler is entrusted by Allah with people but fails to be sincere to them, he will be forbidden access to Paradise." In another narration:

"...If he dies while he is deceiving his people, he will be forbidden entry into Paradise. (Bukhari)

He also (pbuh) said:

"An unjust ruler will receive the severest punishment on the Day of Judgment." (Tabarani)

He (pbuh) also used to say the following prayer:

"O Allah! Whoever holds authority over my nation and is kind to them, be kind to him; but if he treats them with cruelty, be hard on him." (Muslim)

- Islam has forbidden false testimony and perjury and considered it a deadly sin the insistence on which may lead to disbelief. The Glorious Qur'aan says about righteous servants of Allah, (the meaning of which is translated as):

"And those who do not bear witness to falsehood, and if they pass by some evil play or evil talk, they pass by it with dignity." (The Qur'aan, Ash-Shu'araa, 26:72)

Allah's Prophet (pbuh) asked his companions if they wish him to inform them about the biggest of sins, and when they answered positively he (pbuh) said:

"Ascribing partners to Allah, and disobedience to parents."
He sat up from the leaning position and said: "Beware of false words, beware of false testimony..."

He went on repeating it until they wished he had kept quiet. (Bukhari)

That is due to the hazards caused by such testimony to society, including waste of people's rights and the spread of injustice. It causes harm to both the witness (as it helps him with his injustice) and the innocent victim.

Islam has forbidden gambling and drinking of wine, as well as taking drugs The Qur'aan states, (the meaning of which is translated as):

"Intoxicants (all kinds of alcoholic drinks) and gambling and idols and dividing arrows are only an infamy of Satan's handiwork. Leave it aside in order that you may succeed. Satan seeks only to cast among you enmity and hatred by means of strong drink and games of chance, and to turn you from remembrance of Allah and from worship. Will you then not abstain?" (The Qur'aan, Al-Ma'idah, 3 5:90-91).

The Prophet (pbuh) said:

"One who is disobedient to his parents or addicted to alcohol shall not enter Paradise." (Nasae'i)

In order to obstruct the way of marketing or promoting alcoholic drinks, even without drinking it, the Prophet (pbuh) said:

"Curse be on wine, it's drinker, server, seller, purchaser, presser, the one for whom it is pressed, it's carrier, the one to whom it is carried, and the receiver of its price." (Abu Dawood).

By such a serious threat, Islam seeks to protect the human mind and feelings from being deranged or crippled. Islam does not want man to step down from his human status to a lower one of other unconscious creatures. It is a well-known fact that a drug or alcohol addict will do his utmost to obtain money to purchase drugs or alcohol whatever the means maybe. This may lead him to commit other grave sins. Therefore, Islam called alcohol the origin or source of all deadly sins.

As for gambling, if one wins he will consume another's property or money unrightfully, and the exultation at winning may drive him to use tricks and deceit to win again. If he loses he will waste his money in vain, and he may resort to robbery if he loses all his money in order to play games again and compensate for his loss.

Islam has forbidden robbery because it is the illegal appropriation of others' property. The Qur'aan states, (the meaning of which is translated as):

"And (as for) the male thief and the female thief, cut off their (right) hands as a recompense for that which they committed, a punishment by way of example from Allah. And Allah is All-Powerful, All Wise." The Qur'aan, Al-Ma'idah, 5:38)

The application of this punishment is subject to the following:

1. The stolen property must be safeguarded and the robber comes and breaks into a safe, for example, to steal it.
2. The objective of the thief should not be want of food, drink or dress; otherwise, there will be no cutting of the hand. This is supported by 'Umar's conduct in the year of famine (18AH).
3. The stolen property should be equal to the minimum amount liable to cut the hand.

Some scholars pointed out that no repentance is accepted from the robber until he has returned the stolen property to its owner, but if he is penniless he may ask the owner of the stolen money to relinquish his right before the case comes before the court. This is the verdict for theft. However, if the case is one of armed robbery, then it is the same as highway robbery, which has a different punishment.

- Islam has forbidden banditry or highway robbery, which involves armed robbery, terrorizing peaceful people, or murder, as this causes instability and terror. The Qur'aan states, (the meaning of which is translated as):

"Lo! Those who purchase a small gain at the cost of Allah's covenant and their oaths, they have no portion in the Hereafter. Allah will neither speak to them nor look upon them on the Day of Resurrection, nor will He purify them, and they shall have a painful doom." (The Qur'aan, Ali 'Imran, 3:77)

The Prophet (pbuh) said:

"A person who usurps the right of a Muslim, by swearing (falsely) will be condemned by Allah to Hell and deprived of Paradise." A man asked: "O Messenger of Allah! Even if it is a small thing?" He said: "Even if it is twig of a bush." (Muslim)

That is because this involves wrongfully consuming the rights of another.

Islam has forbidden suicide, as stated in the Noble Qur'aan, (the meaning of which is translated as):

"And do not kill one another. Lo! Allah is ever Merciful unto you. Whosoever does that through aggression and injustice, We shall cast him into Fire, and that is ever easy for Allah." (The Qur'aan, An-Nisa'a, 4:29-30)

The Prophet (pbuh) said:

"If a person kills himself with an iron (knife), he will be in Hell with his knife in his hand stabbing himself there forever. If a person kills himself with poison, his poison will be in his hand, administering it in Hell forever. If a person throws himself down a mountain to death, he will fall continuously into Hell forever." (Bukhari & Muslim)

• Islam has forbidden falsehood, dishonesty and deceit; it enjoins truthfulness, keeping promises and restoring deposits to their owners. It has warned against breaking promises and denying trusts. The Qur'aan says, (the meaning of which is translated as):

"O you who believe! Betray not Allah and His Messenger, nor Knowingly betray your trusts." (The Qur'aan, Al-Anfal, 8:27)

It has also enjoined secrecy as stated in the Prophet's (pbuh) tradition:

"If a man tells you something then turns his head away, what he tells you is a trust." (Abu Dawood & Tirmidhi).

It has encouraged sincerity when giving advice. The Prophet (pbuh) said:

"An adviser is entrusted." (Abu Dawood & Tirmidhi)

I has also associated trust with faith. The Prophet (pbuh) said:

"There is no faith in one who lacks trustworthiness, and there is no religion in one who lacks commitment to his promise." (Ahmad and Baihaqi)

He also (pbuh) said, (the meaning of which is translated as):

"There are four (habits) which, if found in a person, then he has pure hypocrisy. However if one of these traits is found in a person, then he has only one sign of hypocrisy, until he leaves it. The four are: When he is entrusted (with

something) he embezzles; when he talks he lies; when he promises or give a pledge he betrays, and when he quarrels he starts abusing verbally. " (Bukhari & Muslim)

Islam has forbidden backbiting, because it spreads hatred among the members of the society. This is indicated in the following tradition:

The Prophet (pbuh) asked the companions: *"Do you know what is meant by backbiting?"* They answered: *"Allah and His Messenger knows better."* He said: *"To narrate such things about your (Muslim) brother which he dislikes."* One of the audience asked: *"Even if my brother maybe like that?"* He (pbuh) said: *"If such defects are present in him as you say, then you have backbitten him, but if he does not have what you say, then you have slandered him."* (Bukhari & Muslim)

Islam has forbidden resentment and envy because it reveals base motives that drive a person to take revenge to quench the thirst of his jealousy and malice. The Prophet (pbuh) was asked: *"Which is the best of people?"* He (pbuh) said: *"He is the pure-hearted, truthful one."* They said: *"We understand truthfulness, but what is -meant by pure-heartedness?"* He said: *"It means the righteous, sinless person whose heart is free from sin, injustice, malice and jealousy."*

The Prophet (pbuh)has indicated the consequences of envy, for it commonly leads to enmity and hatred. He (pbuh) said:

"Jealousy destroys good deeds as fire destroys wood." (Abu Dawud)

* Islam has forbidden deserting each other, as indicated in the following tradition, (the meaning of which is translated as):

"Do not cut off relations with each other, do not harbor ill-will or envy, and - O servants of Allah – be brethren to each other. It is not permissible for a Muslim to keep away from his brother for more than three days." (Bukhari and Muslim).

* It has forbidden cursing, as stated in the Prophet's (pbuh) following tradition:

"Those person who are addicted to cursing too much will neither be interceded nor witnessed on the Day of Resurrection." (Muslim)

Even with enemies, a Muslim should pray to Allah for their guidance to the right path and he should refrain from cursing them or invoking evil upon them. According to Abu Hurairah, may Allah be pleased with him, it was said to the Prophet: *"O Messenger of Allah, invoke Allah against the idol worshipers."* He (pbuh) answered: *"I have not been sent as one who curses, I have been sent as a mercy."* (Muslim)

- Islam has warned against miserliness, because it considers wealth something that belongs to Allah, and Allah has entrusted it to man to spend it on himself and on his dependants, taking into consideration that his needy brothers have a right to a portion of it. Allah's Messenger (pbuh) has indicated the miser's guilt in the following tradition:

"No cheater, miser or one who reminds of his favor to others shall enter Paradise." (Tirmidhi)

The Great Prophet (pbuh)explained the consequences the epidemic of miserliness spreads in a society by saying:

"Avoid cruelty and injustice, for on the Day of Judgment, the same will turn into several darkness. And guard yourselves against miserliness; for this has ruined nations who lived before you. Miserliness led them to bloodshed and to treat the unlawful as lawful." (Muslim)

- Islam has forbidden extravagance and wasting money. The Qur'aan says, (the meaning of which is translated as):

"And give to the kinsman his due, and to the needy and to the wayfarer. But spend not wastefully (your wealth) in the manner of a spendthrift. Verily, the spendthrifts are brothers of the devils and the devil is ever ungrateful to his Lord." (The Qur'aan, Bani Israil, 17:26-27)

The Prophet (pbuh) said:

"Allah the Exalted has forbidden you disobedience to mothers, depriving others of begging and burying little daughters alive. He dislikes you to carry tales, excessive questioning, and wasting wealth." (Bukhari & Muslim)

- Islam has forbidden excessiveness or extremism in matters of religion. The Qur'aan says, (the meaning of which is translated as):

"Allah desires for you ease; He desires not hardship for you." (The Qur'aan, Al-Baqarah, 2:185)

The Prophet (pbuh) said:

"Give good tidings, not bad; make things easier, not harder." (Bukhari & Muslim)

- Islam has warned against and self-conceit and pride. Allah the Exalted has advised us in this verse, (the meaning of which is translated as):

"And turn not your cheek away (with pride) toward people, nor walk in insolence through the earth. Verily, Allah likes not any arrogant boaster. And be moderate in your walking, and lower your voice. Verily, the harshest of all voices is the braying of the donkey." (The Qur'aan, Luqman, 31:18-19)

The Prophet (pbuh) warned against vanity by saying:

"Avoid vanity." (Bukhari)

He also (pbuh) dispraised arrogance by saying:

"A person who has in his heart an atom's weight of pride will not enter Paradise." One man said: "O Messenger of Allah, a man likes his garment and shoes to be nice." The Prophet said: "Allah is beautiful and likes beauty. Pride is the denial of truth and belittling the people." (Muslim)

He (pbuh) also said:

"Allah will not look at one who drags his garment with pride on the Day of Resurrection." (Bukhari & Muslim)

- Islam has warned against all causes of dispute and separation. The Qur'aan says, (the meaning of which is translated as):

"And hold fast, all of you together, to the rope of Allah, and do not separate." (The Qur'aan, Ali 'Imran, 3:103)

- It has forbidden and warned against mistrust and suspicion, Allah said, (the meaning of which is translated as):

"O you who believe! Avoid much assumption, indeed some suspicion is sin." (The Qur'aan, Al-Hujurat, 49:12)

The Prophet (pbuh) said:

"Beware of suspicion, for it is the most misleading of talks." *(Bukhari)*

Islam ordered us to make sure when conveying news The Glorious Qur'aan says, (the meaning of which is translated as):

"O you who believe! If a disobedient brings you an information, verify it, lest you smite some folk in ignorance and afterwards you become regretful for what you have done." (The Qur'aan, Al-Hujurat, 49:6)

- It has forbidden and warned against bad temper and obscenity. The Prophet (pbuh) said, (the meaning of which is translated as):

"A believer is not one who defames others, one who curses others, nor does he speak in an offensive or obscene manner." (Tirmidhi)

- It has warned against rejoicing over the troubles of others. The Prophet (pbuh) said, (the meaning of which is translated as):

"Do not rejoice over the troubles of your (Muslim) brother lest Allah might save him (by His Mercy) and involve you in the same trouble." (Tirmidhi)

- It has warned against interfering in the business of others when it does not concern oneself. The Prophet (pbuh) said:

"It is part of the excellence of a person's Islam that he should discard that is of no concern or benefit to him either in this world or the Hereafter." (Tirmidhi)

- It has warned against anger. The Noble Qur'aan describes the believers in the following verse, (the meaning of which is translated as):

"And those who avoid the greater sins, and immoralities, and when they angry, forgive." (The Qur'aan. Ash-Shura, 42:37)

And:

"Repel (the evil) with one which is better, then verily he, between whom and you there was enmity, (will become) as though he was a close friend." (The Qur'aan, Fussilat, 41:34)

Ibn 'Abbas explained:*What is meant,by patience at the time of anger, by forgiving after being insulted. If they behave accordingly, Allah will safeguard them and their enemy will submit to them like a close friend.* (Reported by Imam Bukhari)

Abu Hurairah, may Allah be pleased with him, reported the Prophet (pbuh) as saying to the person who requested his advice: *"Do not get angry."* When the man repeated his question he answered several times: *"Do not get angry."* (Bukhari)

- Islam has forbidden despising other people.

The Qur'aan says, (the meaning of which is translated as):

"O you who believe! Let not a group scoff at another group, it may be that the latter are better than the former. Nor let (some) women scoff at other women, it may be that the latter are better than the former. Nor defame one another, nor insult one another by nicknames." (The Qur'aan, Al-Hujurat, 49:11)

- It has forbidden taking what belongs to others in any manner because it involves injustice and corruption for the society. The Prophet (pbuh) said:

"Allah has decreed the Fire of Hell for a person who takes the property of a Muslim through false oath and debarred him from Paradise." A companion asked: "O Messenger of Allah! Even if it may be small? He answered; "Even if it may be the twig of a bush." (Muslim)

- It has forbidden the judge to commit injustice, whether he is learned or unlearned. This is because in Islam a judge is considered responsible for implementation of Allah's Law. Thus his role is of an executive not legislative nature.

Therefore, if he committed injustice he would betray the trust put in him. The Qur'aan states this clearly, (the meaning of which is translated as):

"Whoever judges not by what Allah has revealed, such are the disbelievers." (The Qur'aan, Al-Ma'idah, 5:44)

The Gracious Prophet (pbuh) said, (the meaning of which is translated as):

"Judges are three: One in Paradise and two in Hell. A judge who has known the truth and judged accordingly: he will be in Paradise. A judge who has known the truth and deviated from justice on purpose: he will be in Hell. And a judge who has judged ignorantly: he will be in Hell." They asked: "What's the guilt of an ignorant judge?" He said: "He is guilty because he should not be a judge unless he is a learned man." (Hakim)

• Islam has forbidden a man to lack a sense of honor with his womenfolk. This denotes consent to illicit sexual relationships within his family or close relatives. The Prophet (pbuh) said, (the meaning of which is translated as):

"Three people shall be forbidden access to Paradise: the one addicted to alcohol, a person who disobeys his parents, and panderer who consents to the adultery committed by his wife." (Nasa'e)

• It has forbidden men and woman from imitating each other in their dress and other peculiar habits. According to the Prophet's (pbuh) tradition:

"Allah's Messenger (pbuh) cursed those men who imitate women, and those women who imitate men." (Bukhari)

• Islam has forbidden reminders of a favor of generosity, that is, when you remind someone for whom you have done a favor in a way that will injure him. The Prophet (pbuh) said:

"Beware of reminding others of a favor you have done to them because this makes thankfulness futile, and wipe out reward."

Then he recited the Qur'aanic verse, (the meaning of which is translated as):

"O you who believe! Do not render in vain your charity by reminders of your generosity or by injury." (The Qur'aan, Al-Baqarah, 2:264)

The Prophet (pbuh) said:

"The person who retracts a gift is like the dog that devours its own vomit." (Bukhari & Muslim)

• It has forbidden slandering and backbiting whether through words, acts or signs. The Glorious Qur'aan says, (the meaning of which is translated as):

"Woe to every slanderer and backbiter." (The Qur'aan, Al-Humaza, 104:1)

• It has forbidden insulting each other by nicknames. The Qur'aan address the believers in the following verse, (the meaning of which is translated as):

"O you who believe! Let not a group scoff at another group, it may be that the latter are better than the former. Nor let (some) women scoff at other women, it may be that the latter are better than the former. Nor defame one another, nor insult one another by nicknames. How bad it is to insult one's brother after having faith. And whosoever does not repent, then such are indeed the wrongdoers." (The Qur'aan, Al-Hujurat, 49:11)

• It has forbidden spying on people, looking for their shortcomings and listening to their talks unawares. The Glorious Qur'aan said, (the meaning of which is translated as):

"O you who believe! Avoid much assumption, indeed some suspicion is sin. And spy not, neither backbite one another. Would one of you love to eat the flesh of his dead brother? Yet you abhor that! And keep your duty (to Allah). Indeed Allah is oft-Forgiving, Most Merciful." (The Qur'aan, Al-Hujurat, 49:12)

Prophet Muhammad (pbuh) said, (the meaning of which is translated as):

"If a person listens to other's talk to their dislike, he will have molten lead poured into his ears on the Day of Judgment." (Bukhari)

• Islam has forbidden carrying tales for mischief. It has threatened the carrier of such tales with the worst punishment. The Qur'aan says, (the meaning of which is translated as):

"And do not obey each worthless habitual swearer, detractor, spreader of slanders." (The Qur'aan, Al-Qalam, 68:10-11)

The Prophet (pbuh) said:

"A person who is addicted to carrying tales will not enter Paradise." (Bukhari & Muslim)

Such spread of slander for mischief may lead to murder, or at least to enmity and trouble. This was condemned by the Prophet (pbuh) in his saying:

"It is not proper for a Muslim to keep away from his brother for more than three days so much that when they meet they move away from each other. The best among them is the one who is the first to greet the other." (Bukhari & Muslim)

It may also lead to suspicion and spying to decide the truth of the carried tales, which involves several sins. The Noble Qur'aan says, (the meaning of which is translated as):

"Indeed some assumptions are sins, and spy not." (The Qur'aan, Al-Hujurat, 49:12)

• Islam has forbidden belittling the weak and trespassing on their rights, whether the weakness is physical (for example, the sick, the disabled and the aged) or financial (the poor and the needy) or if they are under ones patronage. The aims to create a consolidated society dominated by mercy, love and brotherhood. The Noble Qur'aan says, (the meaning of which is translated as):

"Worship Allah and join none with Him (in worship), and do good to parents, kinsfolk, orphans, the needy the neighbor who is near of kin, the neighbor who is a stranger, the companion by your side, the wayfarer (you meet), and those (slaves) whom your right hands possess. Verily, Allah does not like such as are proud and boastful." *(The Qur'aan, An-Nisa'a, 4:36)*

- Islam has prohibited causing a neighbor any harm or "inconvenience" by words or deeds. The Prophet (pbuh) said:

"By Allah, he is not a believer! By Allah, he is not a believer!" He was asked: "Who O Messenger of Allah?" He said: "The one whose neighbor is not safe from his mischief." (Bukhari & Muslim)

He (pbuh) also said:

"If one believes in Allah and the Last Day, he should not hurt his neighbor." (Bukhari)

Islam has elevated the rank of neighbors, and assigned them considerable privilege as understood from the following Prophet's (pbuh) words:

"Gabriel continued recommending me to take care of the neighbor so much that I thought that he would give him a right to inheritance." (Abu Dawood & Tirmidhi)

- It has prohibited causing any harm or loss to heirs when writing a will. This occurs when the deceased falsely writes in his will that he owes someone a debt, just to prevent wealth from his legal heirs. This is made clear in the Noble Qur'aan, (the meaning of which is translated as):

"... after payment of legacies he may have bequeathed, or debts, so that no loss is caused (to anyone)." (the Qur'aan, An-Nisa'a, 4:12)

The Prophet (pbuh) said:

"Allah has decreed for each heir their due, so there is no bequeathal to an heir." (Tirmidhi)

Commandments

The following are some of the injunctions and commandments of Islam:

Islam has enjoined absolute justice in speech and action. The Glorious Qur'aan states , (the meaning of which is translated as):

> *"Lo! Allah enjoins justice and kindness, and giving to kinsfolk, and forbids lewdness and abomination and wickedness. He exhorts you in order that you may take heed." (The Qur'aan, An-Nisa'a, 4:90)*

Abu Bakr, the first Muslim Caliph, on assuming his responsibilities of Caliphate, said:

> *"To me, the strong man among you is weak until I exact what is due on him, and the weak man is strong until I avail him of what is due to him. Obey me as long as I obey Allah in conducting your affairs."*

Justice is a must in case of pleasure and displeasure, towards Muslims and non-Muslims. The Qur'aan says, (the meaning of which is translated as):

> *"... And let not hatred of any people seduce you that you deal not justly. Deal justly, that is nearer to piety." (The Qur'aan, Al-Ma'idah, 5:8)*

Justice is also required when dealing with relatives and non-relatives, Allah said, (the meaning of which is translated as):

> *"And whenever you give your word, say the truth even if a near relative is concerned, and fulfill the Covenant of Allah. This He commands you, that you may remember." (The Qur'aan, Al-An'am, 6:152)*

Allah has commanded us even to use force, if needed, to impose justice. He said, (the meaning of which is translated as):

> *"Indeed We have sent Our Messenger with clear proofs, and revealed with them the Scripture and the Balance (justice) that mankind may keep up justice. And We brought forth iron wherein is mighty power as well as many benefits." (The Qur'aan, Al-Hadid, 57:25)*

In his commentary on this verse, Imam Ibn Taimia, Allah's mercy be on him, said:

"Sending Messengers and Revelation of Books are intended for people to perform their obligations as ordained by Allah in accordance with justice. If one deviates from the Book he will be corrected with iron (i.e. by force)."

• Islam has enjoined altruism and encouraged it because it reflects true love and a sense of brotherhood and has positive implications on the society. It enhances the ties between its members, motivating them to serve each other sincerely. The Noble Qur'aan has praised those who prefer others over themselves in matters of benevolence and benefit, Allah said, (the meaning of which is translated as):

"... and give them (emigrants) preference over themselves even though they were in need of that. And whosoever is saved from his own greed, such are they who will be the successful." (The Qur'aan, Al-Hashr, 59:9)

• It urged keeping good company and warned against bad company. The Prophet (pbuh)has given us an example that clearly shows us the consequences of good company and bad company. He (pbuh) said:

"The example of a good companion and that of a bad companion is like that of one who deals in musk and the blacksmith. The companion of the musk dealer might buy some from him, or at least you might smell its fragrance. As regards the other, he might set your clothes a fire, or at least you will breathe fumes from the furnace." (Bukhari & Muslim)

• Islam has enjoined reconciliation between people in case of dispute. The Glorious Qur'aan states, (the meaning of which is translated as):

"There is no good in much of their secret conferences save (in) him who enjoins alms giving and kindness and peace-making among the people. Whoever does that, seeking the good pleasure of Allah, We shall bestow on him a vast reward." (The Qur'aan, An-Nisa'a, 4:114)

Reconciliation between people occupies a high rank. It is not inferior to prayer, fasting and other forms of worship. In this context, the Prophet (pbuh) said:

"Shall I tell you of something better than the rank of fasting, prayer and charity (Zakat)? It is reconciliation between people, because discord is an exterminator (of society)."

Islam allows lying in cases of reconciliation in order to infuse hearts with love and accord, unite them and protect them from conflicts and separation. The Prophet (pbuh) said:

"I do not count a liar, the man who utters words for the sake of making peace, in war, a husband's talk with his wife, and a wife's talk with her husband." (Abu Dawood)

He (pbuh) also said:

"He is not a liar who brings about peace between people by saying or attributing good words (to others)." (Bukhari & Muslim)

Islam has commanded enjoining virtue and forbidding evil by all means, each according to his capacity, because this would safeguard people against injustice, corruption, loss of rights, and dominance of lawlessness. Enjoining virtue and forbidding evil teaches the ignorant, arouses the dormant from inertia and negligence of duty, corrects wrongdoers and help the righteous. The Qur'aan says , (the meaning of which is translated as):

"... Help you one another in righteousness and pious duty. Help not one another in sin and transgression." (The Qur'aan, Al-Ma'idah, 5:2)

The Prophet (pbuh) said:

"Anybody among you who notices something evil, should correct it with his hand. If he is unable to do so, he should prohibit the same with his tongue. If he is unable even to do this, he should at least hate it in his heart; this is the lowest degree of faith." (Muslim)

The Noble Qur'aan has stated the punishment of those who neglect such a duty in the following verse, (the meaning of which is translated as):

"Those of the children of Israel who disbelieved were cursed by the tongue of David, and of Jesus, son of Mary. That was because they rebelled and used to transgress." *(The Qur'aan, Al-Ma'idah, 5:78)*

The Prophet (pbuh) described the consequences of failure to enjoin virtue and forbid evil by saying:

"The example of a person who obeys injunctions of Allah and the one who disregards these limits is like passengers on a boat who decide by drawing lots as to who should occupy the upper deck and who should go to the lower deck. Those in the lower deck had to pass through the upper deck to fetch water, which caused some inconvenience to the occupants of the upper deck. So they suggested to the occupants of the upper deck to allow them to bore a hole in the lower deck and to draw water without causing any inconvenience to them. If the occupants of the upper deck were to leave the others to carry out their design, they would all perish together; but if they were to stop them from carrying it out they would save themselves and the others." *(Bukhari)*

Islam, however, has prescribed some limits and criteria for enjoining virtue and prohibiting evil. The following are some of them:

1. The one who takes up this task must be knowledgeable about what he enjoins or prohibits.

2. His prohibition of evil should not lead to a bigger evil.

3. He should not do what he prohibits nor should he neglect what he enjoins, as made clear in the Noble Qur'aan, (the meaning of which is translated as):

"O you who believer! Why say you that which you do not? It is most hateful to Allah that you say what you do not do." *(The Qur'aan, As-Saff, 61:2-3)*

4. He should be kind and gentle when he enjoins or prohibits. He should also bear any inconvenience resulting from this task, Allah said, (the meaning of which is translated as):

"... and enjoin kindness and forbid inequity, and persevere whatever may befall you. Lo! That is the steadfast heart of things." (The Qur'aan, Luqman, 31:17)

5. He should not resort to spying on others in order to discover evil acts. The Qur'aan says, (the meaning of which is translated as):

"... And spy not." (The Qur'aan, Al-Hujurat, 49:12)

*   Islam has enjoined good manners. The Prophet (pbuh) said:

"Among the Muslims, the most perfect, with regard to his faith, is one whose character is excellent, and who treats his wife with gentleness." (Tirmidhi)

The Prophet (pbuh) has also pointed out the reward of good manners, He (pbuh) said:

"On the Day of Judgment, the dearest and closest to me, as regards my company, will be those persons, who will bear the best moral character. And those among you, who are excessive talkers and are given to boasting, will be the most repugnant to me, and the farthest from me on the Day of Judgment."(Tirmidhi)

*   Islam has enjoined doing kindness, as stated in the Prophet's (pbuh) tradition:

"Show kindness to those worthy or unworthy of it; if you show it to those worthy, then they are worthy of it. But if you do not show it to those not worthy of it then you will indeed be in need of it."

*   It has enjoined giving sincere advice. In this context, the Prophet (pbuh) said:

"(The basis of) faith is sincerity." We (i.e. the Prophet's companions) submitted: "O Prophet of Allah! For whom?" He said: "Towards Allah, the Noble Qur'aan, His Messenger and the Muslims – both leaders and masses." (Muslim)

1. Sincerity towards Allah can be realized by believing in Him, worshipping Him alone, ascribing no partners to Him,

declaring Him free from imperfection in His Names and Attributes, and that He controls the affairs of existence. What He wills shall be, and what He does not will shall not be, as well as complying with His commands and avoiding His prohibitions.

2. Sincerity towards His Book, (The Noble Qur'aan) is realized by believing that it is the word of Allah, revealed by Him, and that it is the Final of revealed scriptures. As well as holding lawful all that is stated as lawful in the Qur'aan and holding forbidden all that is forbidden in it, and considering it as the right path and way of life for Muslims.

3. Sincerity towards His Messenger is realized by obeying his orders, believing what he informed of, refraining from what he prohibited, loving and respecting him, complying with his teachings and propagating it among people.

4. Sincerity to the leaders of the Muslims is realized by obeying them unless they enjoin sin, guiding them to good and helping them with it, to refrain from rebelling against them, to gently advise them, and to remind them of the rights of other people.

5. Sincerity towards the Muslim masses is realized by guiding them to what is good for them in matters of their religion and worldly life. Helping them to satisfying their needs, protecting them from harm, loving for them what he likes for himself, disliking for them what he dislikes for himself, and treating them in the manner he wants them to treat him.

• Islam has enjoined generosity, as it leads to people's friendliness and affection. The Prophet (pbuh) said:

"Two traits are liked by Allah: good manners and generosity. Two traits are disliked by Allah: bad manners and miserliness. If Allah wants to favor a servant of His, He uses him to satisfy people's needs."

The criterion regarding generosity is given in the following verse, (the meaning of which is translated as):

"And let not your hand be chained to your neck (in greed) nor open it with a complete opening (like a spendthrift's), lest you sit down rebuked, denied (and impoverished)." (The Qur'aan, Bani Israil, 17:29)

Allah the Exalted has warned against squandering wealth and going beyond the moderate limits of generosity. He said, (the meaning of which is translated as):

"Give the kinsman his due, and the needy, and the wayfarer, and squander not (your wealth) in wantonness...Lo! The squanderers were ever brothers of the devils, and the devil was ever an ingrate to his Lord." (The Qur'aan, Bani Israil, 17:26-27)

- Islam has enjoined mercy, as stated in the Prophet's (pbuh) words:

"He who shows no mercy shall receive no mercy. Have mercy for those on earth, and Allah will have mercy for you." (Abu Dawood and Tirmidhi)

- It has enjoined kindness and gentleness. The Prophet (pbuh) said:

"Wherever there is gentleness, it beautifies, and from whatever it is removed, its beauty is removed." (Muslim)

- It has enjoined covering the faults of others and alleviating their distress. The Prophet (pbuh) said:

"One who helps a fellow Muslim in removing his difficulty in this world, Allah will remove the formers' distress on the Day of Judgment. He who helps to remove the hardship of another, will have his difficulties removed by Allah in this world and in the Hereafter. One who covers the shortcomings of another Muslim will have his faults covered up in this world and the next by Allah. Allah continues to help his servant so long as he goes on helping his brother." (Muslim)

- Islam has enjoined and urged patience in performing devotion and refraining from prohibitions. The Qur'aan says, (the meaning of which is translated as):

"So wait patiently for your Lord's decree, for surely you are in Our sight." (The Qur'aan, At-Tur, 52:48)

This may mean having patience with one's circumstances and the events of life, such as poverty, hunger, illness and fear. The Glorious Qur'aan says, (the meaning of which is translated as):

"And surely We shall try you with something of fear and hunger, and loss of wealth and lives and crops; but give glad tidings to the steadfast. Who say, when a misfortune strikes them: 'Indeed we are Allah's and indeed to Him we are returning.' Such are they on whom are blessings from their Lord, and mercy. Such are the rightly guided." (The Qur'aan, Al-Baqarah, 2:155-157)

Allah, Glory to Him, has stated the reward of the steadfast, He said, (the meaning of which is translated as):

"Verily the steadfast will be paid their wages without constraint." (The Qur'aan, Az-Zumar, 39:10)

• It has enjoined suppression of anger, and forgivness, especially when one is capable of avenging himself. This will make ties among the members of society stronger, help to remove all causes of hatred and enmity, and lead to great reward. Therefore, Allah has praised those who posses such excellent traits. He said, (the meaning of which is translated as):

"And hasten to forgiveness from your Lord, and for a Paradise as wide as are the heavens and the earth, prepared for the righteous. Those who spend in ease and in adversity, those who control their wrath and are forgiving towards mankind; Allah loves the good." (The Qur'aan, Ali 'Imran, 3:133-134)

Islam has also called Muslims to meet evil with good in order to refine hearts and purify them of enmity. The Noble Qur'aan says, (the meaning of which is translated as):

"Repel (the evil deed) with what is better. Then indeed he between whom and you there was enmity (will become) as though he was a close friend." (The Qur'aan, Fussilat, 41:34)

Aspects of Islamic Etiquette

Islamic Law has introduced and propagated a cluster of public ethics. At the same time, it warned of failure to strictly abide by it, as this will entail punishment in the Hereafter. Imam Muslim narrated that the Prophet (pbuh) said:

"Do you know who is the bankrupt?" They answered: *"A bankrupt person among us is the person who has neither money nor property."* The Prophet (pbuh) said:

"The bankrupt in my nation is the one who comes on the Day of Resurrection with prayer, Zakat and fasting, yet he used to insult, slander, slay and beat others. Thus claimants are rewarded according to their good deeds. If one's good deeds are gone, he is punished for his ill-doings until he is thrown into Hell."

❖ **Dining Ethics**:

1. One should start eating by mentioning the name of Allah and conclude with praising and thanking Allah. He should eat from the nearest side of the dish and use his right hand, because the left hand is generally used for cleaning filth.

Imams Bukhari and Muslim narrated on the authority of 'Umar Ibn Abi Salamah, may Allah be pleased with him, that the Prophet (pbuh) said:

"Mention the name of Allah, eat with your right hand and eat from the nearest side of the dish."

2. One should never complain or disapprove of the food presented.

Bukhari and Muslim narrated on the authority of Abu Hurairah, may Allah be pleased with him, that;

"The Messenger of Allah (pbuh) never found fault with any food. If he liked it, he would eat it, if not he would just leave it."

3. One should avoid eating or drinking in excess quantity, in the light of Allah's saying, (the meaning of which is translated as):

"And eat and drink but do not be excessive."

The Prophet's (pbuh) words:

"The son of Adam (man) has never filled a vessel worse than his stomach. If there is no other way out, then let there be a third for his food, another for his drink, and another for his breath." (Narrated by Ahmad)

4. One should never breath or blow into vessels. According to Ibn 'Abbas the Prophet (pbuh) forbade breathing or blowing into the dish. (Tirmidhi)

5. One should eat with others, not alone, since Allah's Messenger (pbuh) said:

"Gather around your food so that it may be blessed." (Abu Dawood and Tirmidhi)

6. If one is are invited to a meal and wants to take somebody with him, he should seek permission for him. According to Abu Mas'ud Al-Badri, may Allah be pleased with him, a man invited Allah's Prophet (pbuh) to a meal along with four other people. A man followed the Prophet. At the door, the Prophet (pbuh) said to the host:

"This man has come with us: If you'd permit, he will come in; if not he will go back." The host said: *"I give him my permission, O Allah's Messenger." (Bukhari & Muslim)*

❖ **Ethics of Seeking Permission**

There are two kinds of ethics:

1. Those relating to social formalities, as Allah said, (the meaning of which is translated as):

"O you who believe! Enter not houses other than your own until you ask permission and greet their inhabitants..." (The Qur'aan, Chapter An-Nur, 24:27)

2. Those relating to formalities in the home, as Allah said, (the meaning of which is translated as):

"And when the children among you come to puberty then let them ask permission even as those before them used to ask it..." (The Qur'aan, Chapter An-Nur, 24:59)

This is all intended to keep household secrets and protect the privacy of homes, as pointed out in the Prophet's (pbuh) saying:

"Asking permission is intended for protection against what may be seen." (Bukhari and Muslim)

It is advisable not to persist in asking permission as pointed out in the Prophet's (pbuh) saying:

"You should ask permission three times. If you are not admitted, go back." (Narrated by Bukhari and Muslim)

❖ Ethics of Greeting

- Islam has encouraged the custom of greetings among the members of society because it leads to love and friendship. This is supported by the Prophet's (pbuh) saying:

"You will never enter Paradise until you become believers, and you will not become believers until you love each other. Shall I guide you to something that makes you love each other? Spread the greeting of peace among you." (Muslim)

- Answering a greeting is obligatory, Allah said, (the meaning of which is translated as):

"When you are greeted with greetings, reply with a better than it or return it..."(The Qur'aan, Chapter An-Nisa'a, 4:86)

- Islam has also explained obligations in matters of greeting priorities. According to the Prophet's (pbuh) saying:

"A rider should greet a pedestrian, a pedestrian should greet one sitting, and a small number of people should greet a larger number." (Narrated by both Bukhari and Muslim)

In one narration by Bukhari, it is added: *"A young person should greet an elder."*

❖ Ethics of Sitting

- One should greet attendants of the meeting or gathering, as pointed out in the Prophet's (pbuh) saying:

"If one comes to a meeting he should Say: 'Peace be upon you!' Upon leaving he should do the same, for the first greeting is not more important than the latter." (Abu Dawood and Tirmidhi)

- It is not appropriate to ask someone to leave his sitting place for someone else as pointed out in the Prophet's (pbuh) saying:

"Never should anyone of you make someone rise from his place to sit there. Rather make more room for others to sit." (Bukhari and Muslim)

"If someone leave his sitting place then returns to it, he will have more right to it", as stated by the Prophet (pbuh). (Muslim)

- One should never separate two persons sitting together as pointed out in the Prophet's (pbuh) saying:

"It is not permissible for a man to separate two men (by inserting himself sitting between them) unless they give permission." (Abu Dawood and Tirmidhi)

- One should never talk to a friend privately in the presence of a third person as pointed out in the Prophet's (pbuh) saying:

"If there are three of you, never should two of them talk without the third until you mix with other people, for this would grieve the third." (Bukhari)

- Never sit in the middle of a circle or group of people, as pointed out in the Prophet's (pbuh) saying:

"Damned is he who sits in the middle of a sitting group." (Abu Dawood)

- Leave space for others to sit, Allah said, (the meaning of which is translated as):

"O you who believe! When it is said, 'Make room!' In assemblies, then make room; Allah will make way for you (hereafter). And when it is said, 'Come up higher!' Go up higher; Allah will exalt those who have knowledge, to high ranks. Allah is Well-Aware of what you do." (The Qur'aan, Chapter Az-Zukhruf, 43:11)

- It is desirable to suppress yawning as far as possible as it is a sign of laziness, as pointed out in the Prophet's (pbuh) saying:

> *"Yawning is from Satan, so when one of you yawns let him try to repel it as far as possible, for if one utters 'Haa!' (when yawning) the devil will laugh at him."* *(Bukhari and Muslim)*

- About sneezing, the Prophet (pbuh) said:

> *"If one of you sneezes, let him say: 'Praise be to Allah!' And his Muslim brother should say to him: 'May Allah have mercy on you' Upon which he answers: 'May Allah guide you and make you well.'"* *(Bukhari)*

It is also advisable for one to cover one's mouth when sneezing. Allah's Messenger (pbuh):

> *"When sneezing; would cover his mouth with his hand or garment and suppress his voice."* *(Abu Dawood and Tirmidhi)*

- One should avoid belching while sitting in the presence of others. According to Ibn 'Umar, may Allah be pleased with him, one man belched in the presence of Allah's Messenger (pbuh). He said to him:

> *"Stop belching, Those who eat most in this worldly life will be the hungriest in the Hereafter."* *(Tirmidhi and Ibn Majah)*

- The assembly should not be busy with nonsense or void of the remembrance of Allah and useful discussions of worldly and religious affairs. Allah's Messenger (pbuh) said:

> *"Whoever rises from an assembly in which the name of Allah is not mentioned is like one who rises from around a donkey's carcass.And that assembly will be a source of sorrow for them."* *(Abu Dawood)*

- One should not face those sitting with him with what they dislike.

❖ **Ethics of Gathering**

In order to make gathering desirable and repel all that cause people to hate gatherings, Islam respects the feelings of the individuals who gather somewhere. Therefore, Islam instructs its followers keep themselves clean, free of bad smells, and with clean clothing, without things that appear offensive to others. It also instructs them to listen to the speaker without interrupting him and to sit where they find room without stepping over people's neck or causing them any inconvenience by pressing against them. This is supported by the Prophet's (pbuh) saying while addressing Muslims during a Friday sermon:

"Whoever has a bath on Friday, puts on the best of his clothes, puts some scent on if any, then attends the Friday prayer without crossing over people's necks and performs whatever units of prayer he could. Then if he keeps quiet when the Imam ascends the pulpit until he concludes prayer, his prayer will be an atonement for the whole week preceding that prayer". (Abu Dawood).

❖ **Etiquette of Conversation**

- One should listen to the speaker without interrupting him until he finishes talking. In his speech during the Farewell Pilgrimage, Allah's Messenger (pbuh) said:

"Ask people to keep quiet." (Bukhari & Muslim).

- One should speak clearly so that the listener may understand what he is saying. Ayeshah, the Prophet's wife said: "The Prophet's words were so clear that everyone could understand them." (Abu Dawood).

- One should be cheerful and speak pleasantly. This is in accordance with the Prophet's (pbuh) saying:

"Do not underestimate any of your deeds, even to receive your brother cheerfully." (Muslim)

He also said:

"A good word is charity." (Bukhari & Muslim).

Al-Hussain, may Allah be pleased with him, said:

"I asked my father about the Prophet's behavior among his companions, to which he answered 'He was always cheerful, easy mannered and lenient. He was not rough, noisy, vulgar, insulting, or greedy. He used to overlook what he disliked without depriving others of hope or answering them negatively. He refrained from disputing, chattering and curiosity. He spared others from three things: He never

censured, found fault with or spied on them. He spoke only what he hoped he would be rewarded for. When he spoke, his listeners lowered their head quietly and when he was silent they spoke. They never spoke haphazardly in front of him. If one talked in his presence they listened to him until he finished. He used to laugh and wonder at whatever his company laughed or wondered at. He was patient with the strangers who were rude in both their talk and requests.'"

❖ Etiquette of Joking

- Allah's Messenger, peace be upon him, said to his companion Hanzala, who thought that life should be free from fun and entertainment and that he committed hypocrisy when he played and jested with his wife and children

"But, Hanzala, refresh your heart from time to time." (Muslim).

Here the Prophet explained to the man that permissible fun and self-refreshment is desirable for the human soul to regain its activity and liveliness. He (pbuh) also taught them the rules of conduct when joking. When asked about his joking with them, he said:

"Yes, but I speak truthfully." (Tirmidhi).

- Once an old woman came to him and said: *"O Messenger of Allah, pray to Allah for me to be admitted into Paradise."* He (pbuh) said:

"No old woman will be admitted into Paradise." On hearing this she went away crying. He said: "Tell her that she won't be an old woman when she goes into Paradise. Allah, the Exalted says 'Indeed We have created them a (new) creation and made them virgins, lovers, friends.'" (The Qur'aan, Chapter Al-Qamar, 54:35-37).

- The jokes of the Prophet (pbuh) were not limited to words, they included acts as well. Anas Ibn Malik, may Allah be pleased with him, said,

"A bedouin called Zaher used to bring presents from the desert to the Prophet (pbuh) and the Prophet (pbuh) would supply him with provisions when he left. He (pbuh) said about him, 'Zaher is our desert and we are his city.' The Prophet loved him, though he did not have a pleasant face. One day, the Prophet (pbuh) grabbed him from behind him.

Zaher said: 'Release me.' Then he looked behind him and recognized the Prophet, so he pressed his back against the Prophet's (pbuh) chest. The Prophet (pbuh) called out: 'Who purchases this slave?' Zaher said: 'O Messenger of Allah, you will find me not sellable.' The Prophet (pbuh) answered: 'But to Allah, you are not sellable' or he said: 'To Allah, you are so dear." (Tirmidhi).

- A joke should not involve any harm or insult to any Muslim. Allah's Messenger (pbuh) said, (the meaning of which is translated as):

"No Muslim is allowed to scare another Muslim." (Abu Dawood)

He also said:

"Nobody should take his (Muslim) brother's belongings." (Abu Dawood and Tirmidhi)

- Joking should not drive a Muslim to lie in order to make others laugh, as understood from the Prophet's (pbuh) words:

"Woe to him who lies when speaking to make people laugh. Woe to him! Woe to him!"

❖ Etiquette of Condolence

- Condolence has been prescribed to console the dead person's family, relieve their sorrows and alleviate their distress. Allah's Messenger (pbuh) said:

"A believer who condoles with his brother on a bereavement will be dressed by Allah in the robes of honor and glory on the Day of Resurrection".

- There is no specific formula for condolence. However, Imam Shafi'i recommended the expression: *"May Allah magnify your reward, give you solace and forgive your deceased one."*

- It is desirable to prepare food for the family of the deceased as is clear by the saying of the Prophet (pbuh):

"Make food for Ja'far's family as they are distracted by the loss."

❖ Etiquette of Sleeping

- One should mention the name of Allah and lie on the right side when sleeping in accordance with the Prophet's (pbuh) words to Al-Baraa bin Azeb:

"If you want to go to bed, perform ablution as that for prayer, then lie down on your right side, and say: 'O Allah! I submit myself to You, and turn my face towards You, and confide my cause unto You, and take refuge in You, out of love and fear of You. There is no refuge or escape from You except in You. I believe in Your Book which You have revealed and Your Prophet, whom You have sent as Messenger." (Bukhari & Muslim)

- One should not sit up late at night. He should do his best to sleep early unless there is some need or necessity. It is narrated that the Prophet (pbuh) disliked sleeping before the evening prayer and sitting and talking after it. (Bukhari & Muslim)

- One should not sleep his stomach as this was prohibited by the Prophet (pbuh):

"Such manner of lying down is disliked by Allah." (Abu Dawood)

- One should make sure that there is nothing that hurts him in his bedding, as recommended by the gracious Prophet (pbuh):

"When one of you goes to bed, he should clear his bed with part of his loincloth as he does not know what is lying inside after he has left it, and let him say: 'O Allah! With Your name I have laid on my side, and with Your name I raise it. O Allah! If You hold my soul (i.e. take my life), then have mercy on it, and if You return it, then protect it with what You protect Your pious servants.'" (Bukhari & Muslim)

- One should be cautious and ward off the sources of danger. The Prophet (pbuh) said:

"This fire is an enemy to you, so when you want to sleep put it out". (Bukhari)

❖ Etiquette of Marital Sexual Relations

- It is desirable, before cohabitation with one's wife or husband to mention the name of Allah. The Prophet (pbuh) said:

"When one of you cohabits with his wife, if he says, 'In the name of, O Allah! Keep us away from Satan, and keep Satan away from (the offspring) that you may grant us,' Then if a

child is born out of this union, Satan will have no access to hurt his child." (Bukhari and Muslim)

- Private relations between husband and wife must be kept secret, as stated in the following by the Prophet (pbuh):

"The worst in of people before Allah on the Day of Resurrection will be the man who cohabits with his wife or the woman who cohabits with her husband, then either they divulges the secret of the other." (Muslim)

- Allah's Messenger (pbuh) recommended play, flirtation and kissing prior to sexual intercourse as evidenced by his words to one of his companions:

"Don't make love with her unless she has had the same degree of sexual appetite as you, so that you do not discharge before her." He asked: "Should I do this?" The Prophet said; "Yes, you kiss, caress and touch her until you find that she has the same degree of erotic urge and excitement as you, then make love with her." (Imam Ahmad)

- The husband should not pull out until she has finished her sexual desire.

❖ Etiquette of Travelling

- One should return trusts to their owners, settle grievances and debts, and leave their family sufficient provisions. He should never travel alone except in cases of emergency when he find no company. The Prophet (pbuh) said:

"One traveler is one devil, two travelers are two devils, but three travelers make a caravan." (Abu Dawood, Nasa'i and Tirmidhi)

- On travelling, one should choose good company and select one person as a leader. The Prophet (pbuh) said:

"When three people set out on a journey they should appoint one of them as a leader." (Abu Dawood)

- One should inform his family of the time of his return from a journey. He should not return at night as this is undesirable since he might see something he dislikes. The Prophet (pbuh) said:

"If one of you is absent from home for a long time, he should not come back to his family by night".

- In another version of the Prophet (pbuh) prohibited a man from returning home by night. (Bukhari and Muslim)

- He should say goodbye to his family, friends and companions, as the Prophet (pbuh) said

"If one of you intends to set out on a journey, let him say goodbye to his brothers, for Allah Almighty will make in their prayers a blessing for him."

- He should return home quickly after he achieves the objective of his journey. The Prophet (pbuh) said:

"Travel is a piece of anguish as it deprives each traveler (of you) of the facilities of eating, drinking and sleeping. Therefore, when one of you has completed the purpose of your journey he should return home quickly." (Bukhari and Muslim)

- Conduct in the Market

- Among the rules of behavior in the market are those included in the Prophet's (pbuh)words when he said:

"Refrain from sitting in the streets." The Companions said: "O Messenger of Allah, we have no alternative, there is no other place where we can sit and discuss matters." Allah's Messenger (pbuh) said:"If it is so, then in that case, discharge your responsibilities due to the street." The Companions asked what their due to the street was. He said: "Keeping your eyes down, clearing the streets of obstacles, responding to greetings, enjoining virtuous deeds and forbidding evil." (Bukhari & Muslim).

- In another narration he (pbuh) added:

"Helping the aggrieved and guide the lost." (Abu Dawood)

He (pbuh) also said:

"Beware of the two cursed practices."

His Companions asked: *"What are the two cursed practices?"* He (pbuh) answered:

"Answering the call of nature in a public thoroughfare or in a patch of shade." (Muslim)

- A passer-by should refrain from carrying harmful weapons or devices, as enjoined by the Gracious Prophet (pbuh). He said:

"When any one of you happens to go through our mosque or bazaar with an arrow (in his hand) he must grasp its pointed head in his palm, so that none of the Muslims should receive any injury from it." (Bukhari & Muslim)

❖ **Etiquette for Buying and Selling**

- Selling is essentially lawful in Islam because it is based on exchange of benefits between the salesman and the purchaser. However, in case any harm occurs to either party, the deal becomes unlawful based on the following verse, (the meaning of which is translated as):

"O you who believe! Squander not your wealth among yourselves in vanity." (The Qur'aan, Chapter An-Nisa'a, 4:29),

- Once the Messenger passed by a heap of corn. He put his hand into it and his fingers got wet from it. He said to the owner: *"What is this?"* He replied: *"Messenger of Allah, these have been drenched by rainfall."* He remarked: *"Why did you not place this on top so that people could see it? He who deceives is not of me." (Muslim)*

- Truthfulness and clear description (of defects, if any) is required in accordance with the Messenger's (pbuh) saying:

"Both parties in a business transaction have the right to annul it as long as they have not separated. Thus, if they speak the truth and make everything clear they will be blessed in their transaction; but if they tell a lie and conceal anything, the blessing on their transaction will be blotted out". (Bukhari and Muslim)

- Benevolence and fair dealing is also recommended in business, since this is a means of strengthening seller-buyer relations as pointed out by Allah's Messenger (pbuh):

"May Allah have mercy on a person who is easy and courteous when he sells, buys or asks for the payment of his dues." (Bukhari)

That is because Islam wants this ease of dealing and tolerance in matters of selling and buying to save people from panting for material interests that undermine brotherly and human relations.

- One should avoid making oaths when selling, in compliance with the Prophet's (pbuh) instruction, (the meaning of which is translated as):

"Avoid too much swearing during sales, for in the beginning it promotes business, and then it brings only loss." (Muslim)

The above are some Islamic etiquette and ethics, and there are many others that would take a very long time to explain. Nevertheless, it would suffice here to remind that no human affair, private or public, goes without Qur'aanic or Prophetic instruction or guidance that defines or regulates it.

Conclusion

We conclude our book with the viewpoint of two people who embraced Islam.

F. Filweas asserted: *"The West is suffering from a vast spiritual void which no principle or faith could fill to bring about happiness. Despite the affluence there, and the so-called economic prosperity, besides the satisfaction of physical needs of people, the Western man still has a sense of worthlessness in his life. He wonder why he is living, where he is going, and why. But no one so far has given him a satisfactory response. Unfortunately, he has no idea that his remedy is in the right religion about which he knows nothing more than doubts. However, the beginning of a light has started to breakthrough after a few groups of Westerners embraced Islam and Western man began to see men and women put Islam into practice and live up to its teachings with his own eyes. Everyday some people there embrace the true religion. It is just the beginning."*

An American lady, D. Potter, who was born in Traverse, Michigan, and graduated from Michigan University with a degree in Journalism, asserts:

"Islam is the Law of God. It is evident in nature all around us. Mountains, oceans, planets and star move in orbit by Allah's command. They are submissive to the Will of Allah their Creator just as characters in a novel are controlled by its author, since they speak and act in the way planned and determined by him. Allah's will is Sublime Similitude. Thus, every atom or particle in this universe, even inanimate objects, is submissive to the Will of Allah. However, man is an exception since he has been given the freedom of choice, so he has the will to submit to Allah's commands or to lay down his own laws or religion. Unfortunately, he has mostly chosen the second option. People in Europe and America are embracing Islam in large numbers because they are thirsty for peace of mind and spiritual security. Moreover, a number of Christian orientalists and preachers who commenced their campaign to destroy Islam and bring out its alleged shortcomings have themselves become Muslims. That is because the evidence of the truth is irrefutable."

If you have any inquiry please contact one of the following addresses

Germany:
1- Tarag ibn Zyed Germany - Frankfort
Tel: 06997390353 Or 06997390354
Fax: 06997390355
2- Kreis Isamischer Shudenten Heidelberg
- Leimerstr 50 69126 Heidelberg
Germany
Tel: 006221/ 768236 order 451635 –
fax: 06221/ 768064 order763424
3- Von Voigt Am Tiergarten 109A
D-30627 Hannover
Tel: 0049 511 5248538
Mobil: 01745820774

United Kingdom:
I- Markazi Jamiat Ahl-e-Hadith
U.K - 20 Green Lane, small Heath,
Birmingham B9 5DB Tel: 0121 773
0019 Fax: 0121 766 8779
2- Al-Muntada Al-Islami Center
7 Bridges Place, Parsons Green,
London SW6 4HW, UK Tel. 44(0207)
736 9060 – Fax: 44 (0207) 736 4255
E-mail: muntada@almuntada-
alislami.org
3- Jam'iat Ihyaa' Minhaaj Al-Sunnah
PO Box: 24, Ipswich, Suffolk IP3
8ED, UK
Tel. And Fax: 44 (01473) 251578
E-mail: mail@jimas.org

Japan:
1- 40 - 13 HIRAOKA - Cho HACHIOJI - shi,
TOKYO 192 - 0061 – JAPAN
TAWHID MOSQ
2- Japan – Islamic center
I- 16 - 11 Ohara - Setagaya - ku Tokyo -
156-0041 Tel: 03- 3460-6169
Fax: 03 - 3460 - 6105

Finland:
Islamic Cultural Community Of
Finland & Helsinki Islam Center - P.O.
Box 33700100 Helsinki. Finland
Tel: 003589736899
Fax:003589735512

Saudi Arabia:
1- Cooperative office for call and
Guidance in
Al-Bat'ha area (Riyadh)
Tel: 00966 - 1 - 4030251
Fax: 00966 - 1 - 4059387
P.O. Box: 20824 Riyadh 11465
www.islamland.org
2- World Assembly of Muslim Youth
P.O. Box: 10845, Riyadh 11443, Saudi
Arabia
Tel: (966-1) 464-1669 Fax: (966-1)
464-1710
E-mail: info@wamy.org
3- Cooperative office for call and
Guidance in Alraboha area (Riyadh)
Tel: 00966- 1-4916065
Fax: 00966-1-4970126
4- Cooperative office for call and
Guidance in Jeddah
Tel: 00966-2-6829898 Fax: 00966-2-
6829898
P.O. Box: 6897 Jeddah 21452
5- Cooperative office for call and
Guidance in Alkobar
Tel: 00966-3-8987444
Fax: 00966-3-8987444
P.O. Box: 31131 Dammam
6- Cooperative office for call and
Guidance in Jubail
Tel: 00966-3-3613626
Fax: 00966-3-3611234

U. S. A:

1- Islamic Society Of Bravard County
550   Florida ave-Melbourne, Fl
32901 U.S.A Phone (407) 726-9357
2- 8500 Hilltop Road Fairfix, Virginia
22031 Tel: (703) 641-4890
(703) 641-4891 Fax: (703) 641 - 4899
www, iiasa. org
Email - info@iiasa.org
3- The Islamic Center Of Charlotte (ICC)
1700 Progress Lane Charlotte, NC
28205 – Phone # (704) 537-9399 -
Fax: # (704) 537 - 1577
4- AI Qur'aan was - Sunnah Society of
Na - 19800 Vandyke Rd - Detriot, MI
48234
Tel: (313) 893 - 3767
Fax: (313) 893-3748
E-mail: Quransunna @aol.com
5- Islamic Assembly of North America
3588 Plymouth Road, Suite # 270, Ann
Arbor, MI48105, USA
Tel.:(734)528-0006Fax:(734)5280066
E-mail: IANA@IANAnet.org
6- Islamic Foundation of America
PO Box: 3415, Merrifield, VA 22116,
USA Tel.: (703) 914-492-Fax:(703)
914-4984
E-mail: info@ifa.ws
7- World Assembly of Muslim Youth
PO Box: 8096, Falls Church,VA
22041-8096 USA Tel.: (703) 820-
6656 - Fax:(703) 783-8409
E-mail: support@wamyusa.org

Canada:

1- Islamic Information and Da'wah
center International
1168 Bloor Street West, Toronto,
Ontario M6H 1N1, Canada
Tel.: (416) 536-8433- Fax: (416) 536-
0417
E-mail: comments@islaminf.com

Danemark:

1- Det islamiske Trossam find pa fyn.
Odense- Danmark - Qrbakvej
247.5220 Odenes
Tel: 004566106608 -
Fax:004566159117
2- Den lighed & brabreskabfare
(Arhus Branbrand) Danmark
Grimbojvej 15.8220 Brabrand Aarhus
– Denmark, Tel: 0045867552611 Or
004586755161- Fax.004586755261
Or 004586261713

Belgium:

1- Center d Education et Gulturel de
Jeunesss Section foundation AI
haramain Belgigue - 100,Rue de la
limite. 1210 Bruzelles -
Tel: 003222237890
Fax:003222237890

Hollande:

1- Stichting El twheed Dellamystraat
49hs. 1053 BG Amsterdam Holland
Tel: 0031235311816
Fax:0031235311816

Sweden:

1- Istamiska Sunni Centert Goteborg
Sweden General sgatan
2- A - 4150 Goteborg
Tel: 004631843917
Fax.004631843917
Mobile. 0046703353617
2- Islamiska Kultur Foreningen 1 Malmo.
Box. 18003 20032 Malmo – Sweden
Tel: 004640948839
Fax:004640944189 Or004640211703

France:

1- Assoctation chemin Droit 81 Rue
Rocheeliouart 75009 - Paris -France
Tel:01-48221986 (0033148221986)
Fax:01-48221049 (003148221049)

SOME USEFUL ISLAMIC WEB.SITES

www.beconvinced.com
www.islamtoday.com
www.islam-guide.com
www.al-sunnah.com
www.thetruereligion.org
www.it-is-truth.org
www.islam-qa.com
www.plaintruth.org
www.islamunveiled.com
www.prophetmuhammed.org
www.alharamain.org
www.sultan.org
www.islamworld.net
www.islamland.org